tender mercy for a
MOTHER'S
SOUL

FOCUS ON THE FAMILY

tender mercy for a
MOTHER'S
SOUL

by
ANGELA
THOMAS
GUFFEY

TYNDALE

Tyndale House Publishers, Wheaton, Illinois

TENDER MERCY FOR A MOTHER'S SOUL
Copyright © 2001 by Angela Guffey.
All rights reserved. International copyright secured.

Library of Congress Cataloging-in-Publication Data
Guffey, Angela Thomas.
   Tender mercy for a mother's soul / Angela Thomas Guffey.
      p. cm.
"A Focus on the Family book"—T.p. verso.
Includes bibliographical references.
   ISBN 1-56179-904-1
   1. Motherhood—Religious aspects—Christianity. 2. Mothers—Religious
life. I. Title.
   BV4529.18 .G84 2001
   248.8'431—dc21   00-012428

A Focus on the Family book published by
Tyndale House Publishers, Wheaton, Illinois.

The author is represented by the literary agency of Wolgemuth & Associates,
717 Branch Creek Road, Nashville, TN 37209.

Editor: Liz Duckworth
Front cover design: Steve Diggs & Friends, Nashville
Illustrator: Arden von Haeger

Printed in the United States of America

01 02 03 04 05 06/10 9 8 7 6 5 4 3 2

For Paul,

amazing husband,
devoted father,
and
friend of God.

Your precious love and grace
are God's tender mercy for my soul.

Contents

In all their distress he too was distressed,

and the angel of his presence saved them,

In his love and mercy he redeemed them;

he lifted them up and carried them.

ISAIAH 63:9

Chapter One

The Tapestry of Motherhood

We had been there all day, and so almost everybody we knew had gathered. It was about 9:00 P.M., and our friends and family were standing out in the hall having a party: laughing and praying and waiting. Paul and I were on the other side of those walls, right in the presence of God, anxious to see the one He was about to reveal. Nine and a half months of waiting and waddling had come barreling to an end … a few more pushes and she would be here.

The emotion and anticipation of those last moments is etched in my memory but remains beyond my ability to describe. I remember being weary and exhausted and yet having more energy and determination than I had ever known. And then … God finally said, "Now," and the most beautiful baby I had ever seen appeared. That day, May 2, 1990, was for me, the beginning of this precious season of life called motherhood.

"Love at first sight" would be a puny description for the overwhelming love that came in and possessed me. Paul was captured by the same love, a love we had never known before, a depth of love that surprised and moved us by its sheer magnitude and power. And now, nine years and three more babies into these days of parenting, we continue to be amazed at how the Lord transforms our lives by continuing to deepen our love for these children.

We heard other parents gush and extol the virtues of parenting before we had children, but I think one is completely unable to process this kind of love and devotion apart from experience. Try as we might, we could not have fathomed how our lives would change, how our hearts would soften, and how God would pour out His goodness through our family. Without question, becoming a mother has been my greatest blessing on this earth.

Most of us are just plodding along, minding our own lives, when we get this wild idea that we are ready to be mothers. The next thing you know, little babies start showing up at the hospital and coming home with you. No one ever asks if you are clear on the instructions or if you have had any training. It is just assumed that you will figure it out. Before you know it, there is a whole minivan full of people who look like you and your husband. And one day you wake up to realize that you are smack in the season of parenthood. That's where we are—right in the middle of the craziest, most labor-intensive, exhilarating thing we have ever done.

And I am like most every other mom I have met: I want to do a great job. I want to be the best mom ever to stir up a batch of brownies. Some days I even begin thinking that I am Supermom: able to do all things in my own strength, able to leap every obstacle in a single bound, able to love and give until I am completely empty.

But these years have taught me the harsh truth about Supermom wanna-be's. They fail. They do not fail for lack of trying, because many go to their graves still trying to do more. They fail because they have misinterpreted the calling. The calling of motherhood is not to be a supermom; the calling is to be a woman of God to your children.

A lot of us operate from some unwritten list of requirements for great mothering:

Love your husband. Check.

Love your children. Check.

Manage your home. Check.

Care for your soul. Huh?

This book is about caring for your soul in the season of motherhood. That's right—caring for *your* soul. Most of us haven't really thought about it lately, but the ache in your heart that will not go away is your soul crying out for attention. I know it sounds impossible. I know that your life is incredibly busy. I know that your children are the busiest children ever born. But it is imperative that we *stop* and find Jesus in all of this.

What scares me more than anything is the thought of waking up in about 20 or 30 years and realizing that I have missed it. I don't mean missing a baseball game or a school play. I mean completely missing the whole purpose of belonging to Jesus.

Too many of us have had children and watched our spiritual lives come roaring to an almost imperceptible creep. We still pray and go to church. But spiritually speaking, we are coasting—downhill. I don't want to coast. I want to grow. I don't want to stick my spiritual head in the sand and come up for air after the last child goes off to college. I can't believe that's what Jesus intended for women.

There is precious counsel and comfort that comes from intimacy with the Father. I need that now. There is great, great joy that comes from fellowship with my Savior. I need that now. Because I hang around the nursery at church and talk to other moms of all ages, I believe that you might be a lot like me: You need to care for your soul.

I know that if my soul is full of the presence of Christ and I am walking by His magnificent strength, then I have more to give to my family. I am a better mother when I am reading my Bible, praying with consistency and power, and pursuing my passions and gifts.

When I hunger for His truth and long for time alone with Him, then I can love my family from the abundance of His love in me. I am not empty. I am not pretending. I am not just surviving. If I am truly *living* in grace and contentment, then my family is living a contented life in a gracious home.

My beloved professor, Dr. Howard Hendricks, taught me many things that have changed my life, but one true thing he said to our class is, "We cannot impart what we do not possess." If I am not crazy in love with Jesus, then how can I expect that my children ever will be? If I do not laugh with them, then who will teach them to laugh? I cannot give to my children what I do not possess. Only in Christ will I have more to give.

The Tapestry

I have come to think of motherhood as a beautiful tapestry woven with many threads of blessing and quite a few strands of frustration. The demands of being a mother can engulf every part of who you are, and the never-ending questions will cause you to doubt your ability. The pattern of the tapestry is intricate, and great skill must be acquired to craft such a priceless work. At times the assignment seems daunting and overwhelming—and it is, when we go it alone.

If there is anything I know for sure, it is that Paul and I cannot do this work by ourselves. Our Creator never expected us to. He wants us to depend on Him for all wisdom. Our sweet Jesus is the giver of all grace. He is the Master Designer and we become capable tools of parenting when entrusted to the Father's hands.

Let's explore the cords which are woven through this unique season.

The Threads of Blessing

In motherhood, God has unveiled the rest of my soul. I didn't have any idea what was inside me. I didn't know that God had built into me the capacity to love so unconditionally, to give so freely, and to protect so fiercely. I honestly didn't think I could do it.

Before my own babies, I had never enjoyed baby-sitting and I wasn't naturally attracted to other people's children. I was afraid that I lacked all maternal instincts. But God proved to me that He had made me for more. After the birth of our first child, slowly but surely, God gave to me every instinct I needed—the ability to discern my own baby's cry, an innate understanding of her needs, and the confidence that comes when you are the only one who can give your child comfort.

The blessings of motherhood have been honored through the ages. Somewhere inside of us, God has told us that this assignment and these relationships surpass any calling on earth. Somewhere in your soul, you know that to hold your own baby and kiss the back of his neck is a holy privilege. The blessings of motherhood are the kinds of things that take your breath away—the moments you hold in your heart forever.

One day someone asked me, "What are the three hardest things about having four small children?"

I quickly responded, "No sleep, the never-all-folded laundry, and talking to little people all day."

Then he asked, "What are three of the best things?"

I immediately realized that the blessings came attached to the frustrations. "The best things are having my three-year-old crawl into the middle of our bed around 2:00 A.M. and hold my hand the rest of the night ... clean-footed pajamas on freshly bathed toddlers, scooting around the house until bedtime ... and the tender words that come from the pure heart of a child."

Like little William, our loud and fun-loving child who, after a few minutes of silly dancing, intently prayed over his lunch, "Thank You, God, for dis bootiful life." Now, that's it for me. Others may run after awards and trophies, but to hear my child thank God for his beautiful life—that's all I need. I will hold his words in my heart forever. I am blessed.

Soul Blessings

It is amazing how God has used these four children to change me in the depths of my soul. The gift of their lives and my changing role as their mother is shaping me in profound ways. There were hidden compartments in my soul that my children have tenderly opened and shown to me: places I had not been, nor could have gone without them.

The fruit of the Spirit from Galatians 5:22-23 has been redefined to me through the eyes and experience of motherhood.

Love. Finally … finally I know what it means to love someone without reference to who they are or what they become, without regard for their accomplishments or the mistakes they have made, without the slightest concern about their appearance or position. Love is that desperate yell for "Mom" that changes into laughter when he finds you. Love is my frantic search for a missing toddler and the tears that well up when I see her. Love is ice cream for breakfast when his throat hurts. Love is a crying child who falls right to sleep in the comfort of my arms. Love is a messy house, a lot of laundry, and pizza on paper plates at our picnic on the floor. Love is different now; it's deeper, unpretentious, indisputable.

Joy. My joy has become more pure, defined by moments, not things. Joy is the six people of our family sitting on our king-sized bed, talking and tickling before we pray. Joy is the belly laugh of a three-year-old, completely taken by his ability to make pig noises. Joy is a trip to the library, fresh snow on the lawn, the first day at the beach, and fireworks. Joy is watching them taste the first strawberries from our garden. Joy is about celebrating the simple beauty that God has woven into our lives.

Peace. Peace is not about stillness anymore. It has become a state of my heart—the calm assurance that comes from being with the people I love. When we are together and safe, in whatever circumstance or difficulty, then there is great and abiding peace.

Patience. I never believed that I would have the patience to potty-train a child or teach my five-year-old to tie his shoes, but I have. I couldn't imagine having enough patience to live through science fair projects or complicated word problems again, but I have. Patience is about letting children enjoy being their age, allowing them to dawdle because they are little kids who need to linger over a bug and spend extra time touching every book on the shelf.

Kindness. I am the person who would have taken the last chocolate chip cookie for myself. In motherhood, I have become the person who will divide the last treat and give it to the children. Where did this woman come from?

Goodness. Goodness requires pure motives. *What would honoring God in our home look like? What would it sound like? How does a "good" mom respond to her children?* My children are God's instruments for tuning this mom's heart and making it good.

Faithfulness. Faithfulness is finally understanding what "I'll love you forever" means—and living it.

Gentleness. Gentleness is about lullabies, sung again and again to soothe the restless heart. Gentleness is about the new-found ability to kiss and make everything better. Gentleness is doing French braids, making paper airplanes, and letting every child stir the waffle mix, even when you're in a hurry.

Self-control. Self-control is the God-given capacity to stop and wait instead of rushing ahead. To wait while my 10-year-old drops an egg on the floor, cleans it up, and then tries again. To wait with a cheerful heart when the children want to "help" fold the clothes a hundred new ways. Self-control is stopping to listen when I don't feel interruptible, and then waiting until all the tears have been dried. Self-control has never been my best thing, but God is amazing. He is using little children to shape my spirit.

The String of Demands

Sometimes Paul will come home from work around 6:30, and little does he know that he is entering the Twilight Zone. I am finishing up dinner on the stove and holding off the swarm of starving children by saying things like "Do not open that refrigerator one more time ... Nothing else until dinner ... No, you may not have a yogurt, we're getting ready to eat." Everyone is grumpy from food deprivation and sibling over-exposure. We're trying to finish homework, clear off the table, hold the crying baby, answer the phone, and all the while Barney is singing "I love you" for the four-hundredth time (at least it feels like it). Paul comes in from a long day in an adult world, and if he has that "What's going on?" look on his face, I immediately begin singing at the top of my voice, "Welcome to my world. Won't you come on in?"

Crazy as it is, this is my world; this is the world that I chose. We begged God to let us have every one of these

Cleaning your house while your kids are still growing is like shoveling the walk before it stops snowing.

—PHYLLIS DILLER[1]

pumpkins. We really wanted to have children. We still want these children. But the truth is that some days, mothering is very, very demanding. Maybe it's not just mothering; it's mothering plus living in this world—this fast-paced, over-involved, politically correct, morally corrupt world. It's trying to balance your children with your career, church, sports activities, social obligations, and the desire to have your neighbors over for dessert sometime.

I hear your wise advice already: "Angela, just focus on your family and let the rest of it go!" I agree, and I have in many ways. But I talk to moms every day who are cutting out every activity they can, and at the end of the day, they still find themselves physically exhausted and spiritually bankrupt. The predicament is that God has put us here, on earth, in these years, and while we can filter out some of the undesirable aspects, just parenting in these times is a formidable task.

Mothering makes full-time graduate school and a part-time job sound like a cakewalk. What was I thinking all those years ago, whining to myself about papers due and final exams? I look back and wince at my lack of perspective. I didn't know what tired was until I had four babies in seven years. I didn't know what arduous meant until I had spent two hours at the grocery store with four children under eight. I didn't know much before I had children, which is just as well.

My friend Nicole Johnson performs a monologue that she wrote entitled "Motherhood." At the beginning of her hilarious and touching drama, she says, "Motherhood is hard. I wish someone had told me that ahead of time. I mean, really told me that. Like sat me down, looked me squarely in the eyes, and said, 'You might not survive this!'" Every time I've watched her do that sketch, the mothers in the audience just roar, myself included. We're laughing through our tears because it's true. Some days it really feels as if we might not survive.

Knowing that a string of demands comes with the job of mother doesn't make them any easier. Those cords get wrapped around every part of our being: our emotions, our spirits, and our minds. Oprah Winfrey has said, "I think that being a mother is the hardest job on the face of the earth." Every woman who has been a mother would loudly "amen" her remarks. Mothering is the hardest job on earth, and it gets harder with every generation.

When I was a child, we went outside to play. We played in the woods, walked to the store, built forts, rode our bikes everywhere, and came home when it was time to eat or when it got so dark we couldn't play kick-the-can anymore. Now, my children can't go in the front yard without me. For their safety, it is mandatory that I am there to watch them. We love to ride bikes and play in the front yard, but that means that nobody is in the house doing the laundry or making dinner. I think back now and realize that my mom probably loved having us run around outside all day; we got tired, and she got a few things done.

Paul and I will never be able to parent as my parents did. Our new society requires that we be superinvolved, hands-on, even a bit overprotective, with our guards continually up and ready to defend against anyone who might bring harm to our children. We cannot blindly place our trust anywhere. We must take authority over the care, the education, and even the play of our children. I gladly do so, but it is demanding, and I am still learning how to balance it all. We must ask ourselves, "How would God have us mother our children in these days? How would He have us balance the demands and stay sane through it all?"

The Strands of Frustration

What is the most frustrating thing about motherhood? The strands are different for each of us, but I do know that all the noise has to rank pretty high. It's loud in our family. Sometimes it is fun-loud and other times it is crying-loud, but every once in a while, it's that shrieking, screaming kind of loud—the version of loud that comes up behind you and makes you jump out of your skin, causing every muscle in your face to twist and contort, forcing you to bellow through clenched teeth, "Cut it out!"

Being a mom is also very sticky. Every day I touch or sit on something that has kid goo on it. You know the stuff I'm talking about. Just today it was two-day-old orange juice that had been spilled under a basket on the floor in the kitchen, some kind of pudding or chocolate stuff melted all over the umbrella stroller, a lollipop sucked and dripped down the face and clothes of our 18-month-old, and an assortment of candy and gum pieces found in a pants pocket after drying. Yuck.

I can handle loud and sticky most of the time, but there are bigger frustrations that come with mothering—spiritual frustrations—the kind of things that take the wind out of your sails and drain your soul. It is these frustrations that drive me to my Jesus, crying out for His provision and His healing.

Exhaustion
I am looking forward to heaven, where I will catch up on my sleep. I have decided that as long as we have children at home, someone will always be up in the night. We don't have a new baby anymore, and I am still up several times a night

for one reason or another. Besides the all-nighters when half the house is sick at one time, it seems that my children need to move around after it gets dark. They come and get in our bed. I take them back to their beds. They come back in an hour to announce bad dreams, lost blankies, and hunger pains.

Like nothing else, fatigue will quickly steal my joy and make me grouchy. I function at half speed and feel frustrated because I cannot get more accomplished during my day. And then there is the monotony. Nothing fuels exhaustion like doing the same things over and over. When someone asks me, "What have you been doing all day?" I say that I do the same thing every 30 minutes: change the same diapers, fold the

With two sons born 18 months apart, I operated mainly on automatic pilot through the ceaseless activity of their early childhood. I remember opening the refrigerator late one night and finding a roll of aluminum foil next to a pair of small red tennies. Certain that I was responsible for the refrigerated shoes, I quickly closed the door and ran upstairs to make sure I had put the babies in their cribs instead of the linen closet.

—MARY KAY BLAKELY

same clothes, pick up the same toys, and feed the same children. Monotony plus exhaustion is a frustrating combination that takes its toll on mothers. Physical exhaustion eventually becomes exhaustion of the spirit.

Emptiness

No one ever told me that mothering would require more than I possess, that at the same time it would be energizing *and* draining. Mothering has strengthened me as a person and yet challenged me right to my core. Loving my children can fill me up, but some days, it will completely empty my soul. To raise children means that you are constantly giving—all of your energies, all of your emotion, all of your time. Often I realize that my well is empty, my mind is numb, and my heart is heavy. There is nothing left for anyone. I am given out.

Identity

I did not know that being a mother would change me forever. In motherhood, I don't even recognize myself anymore; I am some new version of who I used to be. I kind of resemble me, and sometimes I sound like me, but this new person has lost all sense of fashion and vocabulary.

A few weeks ago I went by myself to a department store. I was going to look for a new suit. I took the elevator up and immediately walked straight to the children's department. I wandered around for a good while before I finally remembered that I had come to buy something for myself. The next few hours in the women's department were agonizing. I don't even know what I like anymore. If it's not khakis and a shirt, I am lost. I used to be a really pulled-together, get-it-all-done type of woman—organized, always thinking, balancing and multitasking—but the demands of a family have radically changed me. I am distracted at least every 10 to 20 seconds by something or someone. I forget things, lots of things. I can go to the grocery store for peanut butter and come home with $50 worth of food, but no peanut butter.

I feel lost in the real world. I love to read the paper. It is one of my favorite things, but I get to it at most once a week. I hear other people talking about books and films, events in Congress or state politics, new restaurants and plays, and it all seems foreign to me. The transition of my identity has been frustrating. I know that eventually I will be able to re-enter the world of the educated and well spoken, but for now, this is my place: finger paints and Duplo blocks, soccer games and Rice Krispie treats.

Guilt

The greatest burden to come from the supermom fantasy is the sometimes-lifelong battle with guilt. I wrestle with the ever-present feeling that I could and should be doing everything better. I should make cookies more often. I should read to every child every night. I should make scrapbooks. I should be in their classrooms more and be available to go on all the field trips. I should pray more, sleep less, look better, exercise, and all in all, just be more fun. For as many areas as there are in my life, there are opportunities to feel guilty.

Guilt is a great weapon in the hands of Satan. He uses it to rob mothers of their joy and move them into more "doing" instead of "being." I feel the attacks and it tears the life out of me. As I look into the kitchen right now, I see two piles of laundry on the table. I could feel guilty for spending these quiet moments writing and get up and fold clothes. But then Satan wins; instead, I am choosing my passion, a subject we'll look at deeply in chapter 9.

Spiritually Barren

Mothering is about giving. We give at every level of emotional, mental, and physical energy. We give until there is nothing left. Learning to give without hesitation has transformed my life: it has redirected my selfish thoughts and made me more other-centered. It has realigned my priorities and my motives. But to give and give without being replenished is to eventually become barren and dry. I have struggled mightily with my spiritual life since becoming a mother. Inconsistency gives way to frustration, and eventually the whole effort can seem hopeless.

But this, my sisters, is the place where we must summon every ounce of courage we have left. This is the battle we must fight. This is the one that really matters. If we call on the Lord for anything, we must pray Psalm 23 for ourselves and ask the Lord to come and restore our souls. The soul of a woman, and especially of a mother, must be cared for and attended to. This book is my own battle cry, coming from my own desire to know Jesus intimately in these days of motherhood. We cannot possibly love as we ought from the dryness of a barren desert.

The Weaving

I believe that the challenge of mothering is, in the midst of all the giving, the sippy cups, homework, and basketball practice, being a woman who walks with God. The goal is not to have the smartest kids, to do every activity that comes home in the backpack, or to manage your home the way a CEO does a corporation. The goal for your real life is a family who honors God with children who become independent, spiritually healthy adults who love Jesus.

Real life is about days that are organized and days that are disasters. Real life is about baked chicken and spaghetti, and sometimes about filet mignon with hollandaise. Real life is about Christmas trees that fall down, new jobs in strange places, papier mâché volcanoes that melt in the rain, and a few pans of burnt cookies.

Read Delia Ephron's words about the real life of a mom and smile at the resemblance:

A MOM'S LIFE

Take your plate into the kitchen, please.
Take it downstairs when you go.
Don't leave it there, take it upstairs.
Is that yours?
I'm talking to you.
Just a minute, please, can't you see I'm talking?
I said, don't interrupt.
Did you brush your teeth?
What are you doing out of bed?
Go back to bed.
You can't watch in the afternoon.
What do you mean, there's nothing to do?
Go outside.
Read a book.
Turn it down.
Get off the phone.
Tell your friend you'll call her back. Right now!
Hello, no she's not home.
She's still not home.
She'll call you when she gets home.
Take a jacket. Take a sweater.
Take one anyway.

Someone left his shoes in front of the TV.
Get the toys out of the hall.
Get the toys out of the bathtub.
Get the toys off the stairs.
Do you realize that could kill someone?
Hurry up.
Hurry up. Everyone's waiting.
I'll count to ten and then we're going without you.
Did you go to the bathroom?
If you don't go, you're not going.
I mean it.
Why didn't you go before you left?
Can you hold it?
What's going on back there?
Stop it.
I said, stop it!
I don't want to hear about it.
Stop it, or I'm taking you home right now.
That's it. We're going home.
Give me a kiss.
I need a hug.

—DELIA EPHRON[2]

Did you smile at yourself? I take great satisfaction in hearing another woman speaking exactly the same mom language as I do. Moms are a sisterhood of women who speak the same words and live similar lives—real lives filled with good, difficult, and glad.

The question is, will we, as women of God, learn how to graciously endure the hard days and passionately celebrate the good ones? Knowing the peace of God in my real-life journey begins with the condition of my soul.

Here is what I know about myself: I am entirely unable on my own. In my own strength, I will allow worry and stress to penetrate my soul, removing every ounce of strength that I thought was there. In the midst of hard days, I will succumb to the temptation to fall apart and retreat. In my own power, I am great on the good days and hopeless on the hard ones. That is not the life I want. My life with God is about facing the good and the bad through the power of the Holy Spirit. My only option is to walk with God.

This journey is about weaving the threads of blessing, the string of demands and the strands of frustration. And in the merciful hands of my Father, they become the beautiful tapestry of motherhood.

As a woman of God, I must care for the condition of my soul. As a mother, I must set my eyes on the Author and Perfecter of my faith, committing above all things, even the precious gifts of my husband and my children, that my Jesus will come first. I must do whatever it takes to maintain the wellness of my soul—pursuing God with great passion.

His mercies to me will be new every morning, strengthening me for every task and frustration, teaching me how to celebrate life, and caring for my soul. And from that healthy place of grace and intimate fellowship with Jesus, I will be the mother that God has intended; the tapestry will be woven, and I will have more to give. Proverbs 31:28 promises that the mother who fears the Lord will have children who rise up and call her blessed.

My ambition in life is to present the beautiful gifts of my children, complete in Christ, to my heavenly Father. The challenge is to care for my own soul, to personally grow more in love with my Savior, so that I can love them from the fullness of Christ. For when I am walking with God, when I hunger and thirst after His righteousness, then there is tender mercy for my soul ... and I have more to give.

"His mercy extends to those who fear him, from generation to generation."

—Luke 1:50

Praise be to the God and Father

of our Lord Jesus Christ!

In his great mercy he has given us

new birth into a living hope

through the resurrection of

Jesus Christ from the dead,

and into an inheritance

that can never perish, spoil or fade—

kept in heaven for you.

1 PETER 1:3-4

Chapter Two

Eyes to See

I was waiting in the carpool line at Taylor's school when her first-grade teacher came over to our van. "We moved the desks around today, and Taylor is sitting at the back of the room. I think she's having a hard time seeing the board."

I looked at Taylor and she quickly said, "There was a glare on the board."

Mrs. Anderson smiled a knowing smile and shook her head no.

All the way home, Taylor gave every conceivable six-year-old excuse for why she couldn't see the board. She was tired. There was a glare. The teacher wrote with different chalk today. Anything to avoid the obvious.

As soon as we got home, Paul and I began holding up alphabet flash cards to test Taylor's eyesight. We watched with surprise as her three-year-old brother would shout out the letters before she could squint them into focus. With each letter our hearts sank and the truth became clear: She really couldn't see.

Taylor's frustration turned into a river of tears, and from her broken heart came the fear that she had tried to avoid. "I don't want to get glasses. No one else in the first grade has glasses. I'll be the only one." She had known that something wasn't quite right, that others could see better than she could, but fear had kept her silent.

An appointment with the doctor confirmed our suspicions. "She has her mother's eyes," the optometrist declared, "20/200 in both eyes. You won't have to worry about losing her glasses. She'll probably never take them off."

"How long has this been going on?" I asked. "How can she do well in school if she can't see?"

"She has probably needed glasses for a while but kept her grades up by overcompensating, pretending, and working harder to keep up with everyone else."

Our next stop was the mall and a one-hour lens maker. We selected a frame and came back in an hour. When Taylor's name was called, all the technicians and lab workers came over to watch. I'm sure I had a "What's going on?" look on my face because the clerk explained, "Your daughter has a very strong prescription for her age. We love to watch the expression of a child when she has never been able to see clearly and, for the first time, our work gives her eyes to see." The lab tech fitted her glasses and stepped aside. Taylor's face lit up, and she began reading signs and sale posters all over the store.

She couldn't stop reading. She read every sign in the mall and everything she could find outside. When we got in the car, she looked at the clock and proclaimed with newfound authority, "It's 5:27."

"You've never been able to read that before?" I asked.

"No, ma'am. Hey, look at that," she said as she stared at the speedometer: "0, 10, 20, 30, 40, 50."

"You couldn't read that either?"

"No, ma'am."

It was my turn to cry.

All this time, I thought she could see and she thought she could see, but now we knew she had been missing everything. She read the billboards, every direction sign, and every road sign from the mall to our house. All she had ever known was a dreamy view of the world, but that day was like waking up; images became sharper, colors became bolder, and the sun shone brighter in her world. She hadn't known there was more. She hadn't known that life could be better. But there she was—looking at the same old things with brand-new eyes, feeling incredibly awake and alive—thrilled to be the only girl in the first grade to wear glasses. That day we thanked God for His gift—the gracious gift of eyes to see.

The significance of those days wasn't lost on me. The Lord spoke to my tenderized heart: "Angela, there is so much more to this life, but your eyesight is blurry. You think that you see clearly, but without spiritual eyes to see, you will miss the blessings. You will grope around in the dark searching for My will for your life. You will miss the beauty I have created. You will miss your purpose. You will miss the strength that comes from My power. You will miss the joy of seeing My glory."

Perhaps you are like me and you know that there is more to this life than what you are seeing. The Holy Spirit speaks to your heart and tells you that life can be an exciting adventure of personal growth and deep relationships. There is a better attitude to have. There is character to develop. There are passions to pursue. There is grace, rest, and amazing hope. But in this season, in this laundry and carpool and "What's for supper?" season, our vision has become blurred, life is out of focus, and we are squinting just to get through the day, hanging on until we can fall into bed.

I am right there with you, having walked that path. Many

times I still do, but I absolutely refuse to settle for a shadowy version of the life God intended. I believe that it is the Lord's great desire to give us eyes to see. I believe that He is calling us to fall into His everlasting arms and rest in His compassionate mercy. I believe He is shouting to us that we cannot possibly live this life apart from His power and His presence. I believe that He is saying, "I am here. Hold out your cup and enjoy My love for you."

I pray also that the eyes of your heart may be enlightened in order that you may know the hope to which he has called you, the riches of his glorious inheritance in the saints, and his incomparably great power for us who believe.

—EPHESIANS 1:18-19

Like Taylor in her fuzzy world, most of us exist with a fuzzy awareness of the importance of our souls. Our spiritual lives may be blurry and without focus, but that is not God's design for our lives. We avoid the obvious ache in our hearts—our souls' cry for more—hoping that it will just go away on its own. The fear of finding out that we really are spiritually empty has kept us silent. And so, we have become professional pretenders, overcompensating for our lack of intimacy with the Father. I call it spiritual squinting. But God loves us so much. He wants to improve our vision. He wants to give us eyes to see.

God's Design

God called each of our souls into being and breathed His Spirit into us to give us life. Job 33:4 says, "The Spirit of God has made me; the breath of the Almighty gives me life." We are His precious creation designed for communion with Him. There is no way to fulfill the true destiny of your life, to be the woman God dreamed of when He thought of you, apart from His indwelling. Your soul is the place God fashioned for His presence—the place where He intends to abide and to work. Your soul is a holy place. You were made for God.

Ephesians 1:4-5 says, "For he chose us in him before the creation of the world to be holy and blameless in his sight. In love he predestined us to be adopted as his sons through Jesus Christ, in accordance with his pleasure and will."

We are designed to function poorly, to feel overwhelmed and alone apart from our relationship with Jesus. We are made to be lost without God. If you look to yourself or some worldly effort to fill your soul, then you are left empty because your soul was formed as God's dwelling place. Your soul cannot function as intended apart from the divine and supernatural indwelling of God.

Most of the time, my spirit is the fragrance of my soul—the indicator of how things are going. Am I full of the presence of Christ and acting out of a righteous place, or am I walking in my own strength, flawed and separated from my Lord? My spirit always tells the truth. When I am anxious or nervous, I know that my soul needs attention. When I am bitter or resentful, the truth is that my soul is empty. When I am overcome with self-pity and doubt, my heart is really screaming for intimacy with my Savior.

There is depth to your soul—perhaps more than you can

see right now. God wants to unveil so much more. There is an urgency in these years for you and your family. *Doing* is not *being*. Surviving is not truly living. Your soul must be protected, attended to, and cared for. Do you sense that too many years have already gone by and too many opportunities have already passed? Now is the time; these are the days to begin caring for your soul.

Our Blurred Vision

I was talking to a mom last week, and after we spent a while comparing gymnastics schedules, I asked her, "In your busy life, how do you find time to care for your soul?"

She immediately responded, "I don't. My children are my life. I divide my time between work, being a room mom, three hours of gymnastics every day, meals, and taking care of our home."

We both looked at each other with sad eyes, not sure of what to say or where to begin. I finally said, "Carman, those are good and noble things, but what about caring for your soul?"

She tearfully agreed. "I know. I am way past knowing. I am hurting."

Bryan Chapell tells a poignant story about the blurred vision of motherhood in *The Wonder of It All*:

She took her children to the park to break the monotony of summer days, and instead she broke her own heart. She watched her children run to the playground equipment as another car drove into the parking lot. The new car ground to a quick stop. A young, attractive woman with a beaming smile leaped out of the driver's seat and virtually skipped to the secluded picnic table near an adjoining lake.

The imagination of the mother began to race. Who could this attractive young woman be meeting in such a secluded spot with so much enthusiasm? Was this a date or a tryst between secret lovers? The young mother determined to stay on the lookout for whoever got out of the next car.

No one else came immediately. The mother soon grew preoccupied with her children and forgot to watch the young woman. When she did finally glance again at the secluded woman, what the mother saw made her own heart hurt. The woman was reading a Bible. The person she had leapt from the car to meet with such enthusiasm was the Lord.

The mother recognized with pain that penetrated her spirit that she no longer had that same enthusiasm. Once the excitement of her relationship with the Lord had overwhelmed her. Once the joy of her salvation had burned warm and bright. But the fervor was gone. Faith had become dreary duty; God had become a detached, frowning bystander. Something had happened over the years of her walk with the Lord. She did not know what it was, but she did know that she would not now be one to skip to meet him. She had lost something wonderful, and she wept there in the park for her loss.[1]

If being a mother is the hardest job on earth, and if we are the most overcommitted people on the planet, then it's no wonder that caring for everyone else supersedes almost every attempt to nurture our souls and to pursue spiritual maturity.

We don't have eyes to see from lack of want, because deep in the heart of every woman is a longing for the fullness that only Christ can offer. We don't have eyes to see because we have committed all of our energies, all of our love, all of our devotion, and all of our vision to everyone except Jesus. And in doing so, it has seemed noble, righteous, servantlike, humble, and almost saintly to give to the brink of exhaustion. My mentor says, "Good can be the enemy of the best." In trying to be *good* mothers, have we forsaken what is *best*?

Spiritual Squinting and Other Frail Attempts to See

Occasionally we resolve to do better. We say, "I have to do something for myself," and then we do little things—applying Band-Aids to our hurting souls. We go to dinner with our girlfriends. We light candles and take a long bath with the door locked, pretending that we don't hear the cries or see the notes slid under the door. We call a friend long-distance and talk for a few hours. We read a magazine instead of cleaning the bathrooms. We eat a few pieces of Valentine's candy from the children's party bags. Little indulgences. Little attempts to feed the spirit that hungers inside each of us.

A few years ago I declared, "I am taking a personal retreat." My family agreed that I was needy, and so I began. I worked like a dog to get away—all the laundry done and ironed, food cooked and labeled for every meal, instructions taped to the refrigerator and mirrors—over-the-top family planning.

I went away for two whole days and spent most of it trying to recover from sleep deprivation. It felt as though I blinked twice and my retreat was over. I came home to the crazy house where little people had their clothes on backward, my husband was frazzled, most of the food I had prepared had not been eaten, and everyone who hadn't seen Mommy in 48 hours was desperate for me to love their boo-boos and read them five books. I felt guilty for going, still empty and doubting it was worth all the effort.

I am not finished with occasional indulgence and personal retreats. As a matter of fact, I run toward those moments of refreshment. But I have come to realize, from the ache in my heart, that my soul needs more. I need more than a few hours in church on Sunday and an hour of Bible study on Wednesday. Conferences, workbooks, videotapes, Christian talk radio—they are all great, but I need more.

I need a love that is deeper, lasts longer, and satisfies the hunger inside me. I need a relationship that is consistent and pure. I need someone who knows me, really knows me. I need oceans of strength and mountains of grace. I desperately need Jesus Christ, not just hearing about Jesus, reading about Jesus, or singing about Jesus. I need the Son of God to come and do the Bible in my life.

I need Him to walk around in my soul and open my eyes. I need Him to forgive, restore, and change me into His likeness from encounter to encounter. I need spiritual depth and maturity. I am so needy that this cannot wait until the children are older or until our lives are "settled." I must finally come to the end of myself and cry aloud, "Dear God Almighty, I cannot possibly make it apart from You."

To begin to care for my soul is to admit that my vision has become blurry. My family's schedules are in high gear, so add three meals a day, plus clean laundry for six people, and I am spinning. I can't see God anymore. I can't feel anything except someone tugging on my jeans. I can't hear anything except "Mommy." I am empty. There must be more to living for

God. I am tired of spiritually squinting and pretending. I am weary from overcompensating and acting as if I can see the board from the back of the room, when in truth it has become one big blur. I can't match all the socks and get the clothes put away, much less know God's will for my life.

I know that I must turn to the Physician of my soul and trade my fears for His vision, my hectic life for His peace. It is time to ask for spiritual eyes to see. It is time to change. I can't bear the thought of living like this for the rest of my life. I want to walk with God and enjoy His presence. I want to be filled by His love and commitment to me. I want the fresh vision that comes from intimacy with Him. I want His love to spill out of my life and onto the ones I adore. I truly want the sight that He offers.

The Invitations of Christ

The Great Physician has been waiting for me—waiting for me to admit my deep need and surrender to Him. An optometrist works in his office and waits for patients. He is able to improve your vision, but he will not work until you get tired of squinting and come in.

God is not like the optometrist, because He will pursue you. He is not hampered by the confines of an office. He will be relentless in His compassion and care for you. He is already wherever you are, inviting you to come to Him. He is already working in your life, shouting to you from the vastness of creation that He loves you more than you can imagine.

Your appointment with God is divine and He can see you at any time: no referral needed, no insurance required, no co-pays, no deductibles, no waiting rooms. Just come, anytime, and be seen by Jesus. In Matthew 11:28-30, He says:

Come to me, all you who are weary and burdened, and I will give you rest. Take my yoke upon you and learn from me, for I am gentle and humble in heart, and you will find rest for your souls. For my yoke is easy and my burden is light.

In Scripture, Jesus extends to us two invitations. The first is to come to Him and be saved. Come and yoke yourself with Jesus Christ. Come and find rest from the burden of your sin. Come and trade your busy life for His, because only by the power of the Son of God will there be rest for your soul.

Just think about "rest for your soul." Doesn't that mean that when you come to Jesus, you will be delivered from your fears, every need will be supplied, and your heart will be full of His presence? Of course it does. And so where is all the rest? Why are we spiritually empty? Why do we feel lost and alone? Our souls are aching, either because we have never come to Christ or because we have not stayed.

The second invitation is to remain. In John 15, Jesus says (emphasis added):

Remain in me, and I will remain in you. (v. 4)

I am the vine; you are the branches. If a man *remains* in me and I in him, he will bear much fruit; apart from me you can do nothing. (v. 5)

If you *remain* in me and my words *remain* in you, ask whatever you wish, and it will be given you. (v. 7)

As the Father has loved me, so have I loved you. Now *remain* in my love. If you obey my commands, you

will *remain* in my love, just as I have obeyed my
Father's commands and *remain* in his love. I have told
you this so that my joy may be in you and that your
joy may be complete. (vv. 9-11)

Many of us have come to Jesus for salvation: a life-changing
experience from which we receive forgiveness of sins, the
indwelling of the Holy Spirit, and the assurance of our eternity
with the Father. But then many of us wander away from the
One who has saved us. We have forgotten that He calls us to
come and then to *remain … abide … stay.*

When I invite someone to my home, especially someone
that I love, I don't leave that person standing at the front door
or even in the foyer. If it's someone whom I really want to spend
time with, we always end up in the kitchen, sitting around the
table, watching the children play (and fuss), talking, laughing,
and lingering in the pleasure of each other's presence.

I especially love to go to someone's house for dinner and
have that person hand me something to do. I feel welcome,
needed, and loved. I don't want to sit on the stuffy chair in the
dining room and wait until something perfect is presented. I
want to be in the kitchen, chatting, stirring, and serving.

Many of us have invited Jesus in but left Him standing at
the front door of our lives. We have put Him on the stuffy
chair reserved just for guests. We occasionally acknowledge
His presence with polite conversation but never allow Him
into the kitchen of our hearts. He must be in the center of our
lives, active and involved. Let Him come and abide in you.
Remain with Him. Linger in the pleasure of His company.

To come to Jesus for salvation is only to taste of the pleas-
ures of the Father, but to remain in Him is to eat at the feast
of His goodness until your hungry soul has been satisfied. For

me that means spiritual fullness, a supernatural contentment that wraps itself around every part of my life, a great peace that comes in and ministers to my family, the blessing of knowing real joy in simple moments. To abide with Christ—to stay with Him and to learn from Him—is to continually receive eyes to see, ears to hear, and a heart to obey.

The Sight That Comes from Surrender

Whether you have wandered away or been lulled into spiritual sleep, the answer for your saved, but empty, soul is the same: Run toward God and remain with Him. Bring the empty cup of your soul and the mess. Bring your dreams and your failures. Bring every question you have ever had. Bring everything that has kept you away, and run into the strong arms of Jesus.

To surrender is to give up trying on your own. It is to have attempted life without God, or with only a casual acquaintance with Him, and found it unbearable, miserable, and shallow. To surrender is to know in your heart that you are not enough. You will never make it on your own. You cannot really be a supermom and do everything for everybody and stay sane. Life apart from God defies logic. Remember, we were made by the

Spiritual surrender is not resignation. It is not choosing to care no longer.... It is surrender with desire, or in desire. Desire is still present, felt, welcomed even. But the will to secure is made subject to the divine will in an act of abandoned trust.

—JOHN ELDREDGE[2]

breath of God and designed to live in fellowship with Him. To surrender is to go home … where you belong … with God.

I know that you battle every distraction imaginable. I do too. There is a whole world full of reasons and mild emergencies that can pull me away from Jesus. I could fill up any given day pouring every minute into my husband, my children, my work, or our home. Some of you are squirming already, thinking that I am asking you to add one more thing to your "to do" list. Please hear this, surrender is not something *you* do; it is something that your *Father* does for you. It is about crawling up into the lap of your heavenly Father and resting in His embrace.

Let me describe what surrendering might mean for you:

- Surrendering is letting the One Who Is Able meet you where you are, reach into your life, and pull you close to Him. You do not have to figure out how to do this. He has already been at work in your life, reaching for you. You are the object of His greatest affection, the reason for His longing. He is closer than your breath. Would you see that He is here and rest in His presence?

- Surrendering is not for the strong and the "all-together" but for the weak and the feeble. It is not about doing something great or leading a holy life. Surrender is simply entrusting your life to the Almighty and trusting the One who made you to keep you. The grace that first drew you to Him is the grace by which you can remain. The context of your life may have you spiritually paralyzed; you may be so overwhelmed that you cannot move in any direction. But you *can* call on the strong name of Jesus. He will come and gently take your face in His hands, lovingly open your eyes, and wipe away the tears so that you can behold the glory of His love for you.

- Surrendering is a conscious, deliberate effort to turn from the life you are leading and run toward God. The rest of this book is devoted to understanding how we can run toward Him, but first you must choose—right where you are, in whatever circumstance—to turn your eyes toward God, to stop looking at yourself and your life, and to turn the gaze of your heart toward your Father.

- Surrendering says, "I choose to stay with God. I will remain with Him and trust in Him. When my life gets really busy or days become difficult, I choose to remain in the arms of my Father and let Him hold me. I choose His strength over my own, His patience, His wisdom—I choose God." Hear me on this one, surrender is a daily, sometimes, moment-by-moment decision, an act of your will to stay with God. You can become anxious and squirm to get away, or you can become anxious and choose to stay, trusting in His provision and strength.

For me, conscious surrender involves all kinds of praying. I ask questions: *Lord, where are You in this? How are You leading? How can I love You?* I pray for help: *God, I need Your wisdom ... Please add faith to my heart ... Hold me tight; I'm so alone.*

And then there is conscious waiting to hear from God in my life—giving up my obsession to have an instant resolution for every situation, resting in His might and waiting for His goodness.

When you run toward God and draw near to Him, an amazing thing happens in your soul. God begins to heal and to mend. He starts to fill and to restore. The car blows up, the dishwasher leaks, the children are screaming, and right in the middle of it all, God comes and gives you His peace. It is a supernatural experience.

True surrender is not an easy out, calling it
quits early in the game. This kind of surrender comes only after the night of wrestling.
It comes only after we open our hearts to
care deeply. Then we choose to surrender, or
give over, our deepest desires to God.... The
freedom and beauty and rest that follow are
among the greatest of all surprises.

—JOHN ELDREDGE[3]

When God is near, we act out of the security of His love
and provision and speak encouragement and hope. It is an
awesome moment to sense the presence of God and hear
yourself respond to others from His fullness. He gives you eyes
to see and ears to hear, and then one day you realize that our
precious Father has been holding you tightly. You sense the
power of His love, and you know that you are surrounded by
the strength of His embrace. And right there in the tight grip
of God, you are free, finally free.

What is the condition of your soul? In the midst of mothering, do you continue to grow in godliness? Do you hunger
and thirst after God? Have you stayed or have you wandered?
Are you struggling to hang on through the blur or has the
tight grip of God set you free? Perhaps you are a lot like me
and, among all the good intentions, your sight has become

blurry, your cup has become empty, and you have somehow lost your way.

It's hard to admit our vision is poor. We squint and work around it. We hold the paper further away and strain to read the street sign just as we drive past our turn. We struggle and rationalize until it won't be avoided anymore. Sometimes we don't even realize that we have been squinting until there is something we'd like to see clearly but we can't quite focus. Then we realize there must be more.

God wants you to be able to see your same old life with brand-new eyes. He wants you to know what it feels like to be incredibly awake and alive, to know the thrill of every new truth He has for you and every opportunity He has planned, to live in the joy of His intimacy, and to improve your vision to keep you from stumbling. He wants the world to be brighter to you.

My friend ... my sister in mothering ... my colaborer in loving and nurturing and giving ... let the tender mercy of Jesus fill your soul. Hear again His invitation to give you eyes to see:

> Come to me, all you who are weary and burdened, and I will give you rest. Take my yoke upon you and learn from me, for I am gentle and humble in heart, and you will find *rest for your souls*. For my yoke is easy and my burden is light. (Matthew 11:28-30, emphasis added)

> Now *remain* in my love.... I have told you this so that my joy may be in you and that your joy may be complete. (Matthew 15:9, 11, emphasis added)

Would you choose to come to Him and then, moment by moment, from encounter to encounter, deliberately choose to stay?

For the LORD your God is a merciful God;

he will not abandon ... you.

DEUTERONOMY 4:31

Chapter Three

The Full Cup

*M*aking spaghetti sauce is where this whole thing started. Paul and I had a Tuesday night arrangement. After work, he would fix pasta and care for the children so that I could teach a women's Bible study. My assignment was to make the sauce. One inspired week I tackled a family recipe, and from then on, there was no turning back. Sauce from a jar became a distant college memory.

Seven months pregnant with our third child, I had finally gotten a burst of energy. That particular Tuesday morning, I woke up long before the sun and began chopping and sautéing. I felt so good that I decided to really get in gear and began working on the laundry. By 9:00 A.M., I had done practically everything: the freshly made sauce was simmering; all the laundry was folded and put away; the children had been dressed, fed, and taken to preschool; I was showered and outfitted in a new maternity ensemble.

That day I was as close as I have ever been to being a super-mom. I had everything and everyone in their place. You know the feeling. It's that moment of satisfaction you get when company is coming for dinner and, just before they arrive, it all comes together. All the dirty clothes are safely hidden in the dryer. The dimmed lights make the house look spotless. The meal is ready. The candles are lit. The music is wafting. The children are freshly scrubbed and looking out the window. You know, one of those rare moments—a postcard moment. This was one of those mornings. The house sparkled, I was happy, and it felt wonderful to have my home organized and humming. I remember being proud of my time management and discipline. I felt strong, in charge … invincible.

That morning, Paul was still home and on his way to the office. He rushed down the stairs and began gathering his things as I tried to tell him about everything I had already done for the day. He listened, though distracted, and then hastily said, "That's great," as he gave me a kiss and headed out the door. That was it. Nothing earth-shattering, just a feeble little "That's great." But somehow it broke my heart.

After he left, I stood in my clean house, stirred my perfect sauce, looked at my empty laundry room, and began to cry. *Why am I doing all this? Nobody notices. Nobody really cares. I just want somebody to say thank you. I want to be valued.* Then I became angry at Paul. *I must be married to the most insensitive man in the world. I can't do anything to please him. Doesn't he see how much I do for our family?* I had needed something else that morning—something encouraging, something filling. But Paul hadn't come through and I began to crash.

I spent the next while lying on my bed, grieving the emptiness that had barged into my home and overcome me. Only hours before I had been the picture of efficiency and accomplishment; how could I have fallen so hard and so fast? I cried for my empty life and my desperately empty heart.

How could I teach Bible study that night? Everything had just been drained out of me, and I had nothing to give. I began to play old tapes in my mind. I relived past hurts, justifying my pain. I cried out to God, begging Him to change our circumstances and change Paul.

But God had a different plan that day. Paul wasn't the one who needed to change.

It was me.

The phone rang, and it was our good friend Dr. Jim Smith. All I needed was his warm "What's going on?" to get me started. I was so completely frustrated with Paul, so tunnel-visioned that he was the cause of my emptiness and pain. I unloaded and cried.

Jim had discipled Paul and married us. He and his wife, Karyn, have walked with Paul and me through every growing place of our marriage. We live states away but talk a couple of times a month. Jim and Karyn are safe. They love us purely and freely. Divinely appointed by God, he called in the middle of his work day just to check in. I'm sure he hadn't expected a weeping, pregnant woman.

Jim listened patiently. After a very long time of listening, he asked, "Are you in the kitchen?"

It wasn't the sort of insightful question I had expected from this strong theologian and teacher. He caught me off guard and I had to stop crying to answer, "No," not sure why it mattered where I was falling apart.

"Go to the kitchen and pick up the phone."

What is this? I thought. *It's a good thing I trust you.*

"I'm here."

"Get a glass and stand by the sink."

"Okay."

"Angela, I wouldn't ask very many people to do this, but

you and I think alike, so go with me here. I want you to fill half the glass with water."

I still couldn't imagine what this had to do with anything, but I stood at the sink and ran water into the glass.

"Okay, you are the glass and Jesus is the water. Now talk to me theologically about the glass."

This had to be the dumbest illustration I had ever heard. Hadn't he heard me? I was hurting over Paul, for goodness' sake. What was I doing leaning over my sink, holding a glass of water? Didn't he need to call Paul and make *him* hold a glass of water?

I searched my mind for some great theological insight, trying to think of some big word like *soteriology* or some keen observation to make about the glass. But I was so empty that all I could come up with was, "The water is in the glass."

"Good," said my patient mentor. "Now keep going."

"Jesus is in the glass. Jesus is in me," I squeaked through my tears and the ache in my throat.

"Who?"

"Jesus."

"Who?" he asked more forcefully.

"Jeeeesuuus," I wailed. "Jesus is in me."

"Who is in you, O child of God?"

"Only Jesus."

Jim was holding up new lenses, and I was beginning to see.

"Angela, keep holding the glass and continue to talk to me. Does the water fill completely where it is?"

"Yes," I whispered, looking down at my glass.

"Tell me more."

"The water runs to the edge, filling all the space in the bottom of the glass."

"Are there any holes?"

"No holes. Completely filled."

"Did Paul have anything to do with filling the glass?"

The power of his question made me cry fresh tears of understanding. "No, only water fills the glass. Only Jesus can fill me."

"Yes, only Jesus can fill you. Now hold the glass under the faucet and let the water run into it. Keep talking theology."

"The water is filling the glass. Jesus is filling me. Now the glass is full … the glass is running over.

"What is happening to the water?"

"It's spilling."

"Who is spilling?"

"Jesus is spilling over."

"Why?"

"Because the glass is full."

"Where is He spilling?"

"Everywhere."

"Talk to me about you."

"Only Jesus can fill me completely, and when I am full of Jesus, I am overflowing … spilling onto everyone around me … sloshing out Jesus everywhere I go."

I stood at my sink and let the power of this picture etch itself into my soul. I was holding a glass under a faucet, watching the water run all over my hands and arms, experiencing one of the most powerful lessons of my Christian life.

Jim finally spoke his tender words of truth. "Angela, your expectations toward Paul have been misplaced. Paul is a great man of God, but he can never do what only Jesus can do in your soul. Only Jesus can fill you. Only Jesus can love you completely. Only Jesus will meet every need. Paul is your life partner. He is your friend and your love. He needs your grace. He needs Jesus to spill from your life onto him. You must run to Jesus to be filled. And when you are full, everyone around you gets Jesus—your husband, your children, your friends. You spill Jesus onto them from your full cup."

And to know this love that surpasses knowledge–that you may be filled to the measure of all the fullness of God.

—EPHESIANS 3:19

For the first time in my life, I got it. Most of my life, it had been me *and* Jesus. Me plus the power of the Holy Spirit, my strength plus God's help—together we could do anything. I stood at a sink holding a glass of water and finally understood the grace and truth of the gospel. I am empty without the filling of Jesus—nothing, really and truly nothing by myself. I cannot fill myself with shallow accomplishments and accolades. Paul cannot fill me. And I believe God saved me from expecting that my children could fill up my life.

I cry even now as I write these words. Those moments in my kitchen were among the most powerful I have ever known. The Lord in His great mercy came into my perfect house that day and began to clean up the mess I had made and wallowed in for so long. I have never been the same, never looking at Paul or my children with the same eyes. My sweet Jesus stood with me that day and gently removed the distorted lenses I had been wearing. I am humbled to have had a friend who was brave enough to say, "You are wrong, and you are looking in all the wrong places. May I lead you to the answer? Let me take you to Jesus."

That night, I went to Bible study and confessed to a room

full of women the depth of my sin and the foolishness of my heart: The pursuit of spaghetti sauce and pressed shirts had become more important to me than the condition of my soul. I confessed that I had consciously and unconsciously placed too many expectations on Paul and on myself: perfect house, perfect husband, perfect children. I cringe to recount how completely misguided and desperately empty I had been.

In the process of trying to fill myself up, my soul had become an empty box wrapped in beautiful paper, tied with a fabulous bow. From that night, our Bible study had a new catchphrase, "having a bow on it," which meant to try to cover up the empty places in our lives.

That night with my friends was more than a time of confession. I humbly testified to the gracious love of our Savior and His redemptive pursuit of us—His reclaiming love. He really does come and find us. He uses broken hearts and godly friends to make us look more like Him. He graciously interrupts the perfect to restore the passion. He is faithful to seek out His own and to do whatever it takes to make us into His likeness. He calls us His beloved and mercifully saves us from our sin and from ourselves.

Your Cup

And so, my sister, where do you hold out your cup? Do you expect that your husband will fill your soul? Do you hear yourself say, "My children are my life"? Have you been waiting to start living until you can get your house organized, the carpets replaced, and enough things to make you feel happy? Will one more promotion at work finally fill you up? Have you imposed huge expectations on everyone in your life, waiting for them to fill your cup?

Here is the truth that will set you free. None of those

things, none of the people in your life, not even your awesome husband and your cute children, will ever fill the cup of your soul. Remember, *you were made for God.* Jesus is the only answer for your empty soul. This one great truth has given new life to my marriage, saved my children from years of therapy, and built a spiritual fire in my life. I am telling you, when it finally clicks, when you finally live in the fullness of Christ alone, your life will radically change.

I have a friend who had been a believer for a very long time. After years of spiritual battles and frustrations, she finally came to understand the great blessing of being filled by Jesus alone. She told me how great a change this truth had been for her and says that her life is so much brighter now, "with Jesus in my heart." You see, Jesus had been in her heart ever since she asked Him to be her Savior, but she had tried to add so many things to Him. She came to understand that God's tender mercy for her soul was in Jesus Christ alone.

When you aren't depending on your husband to fill you up, then he can make mistakes and you are still okay. He can say the wrong thing, and you can forgive him quickly. He can struggle and question his direction, and you don't fall into despair. He can be your partner and your friend, because he does not have to be your Savior.

When you are living in the fullness of Christ, your children are being sloshed with His grace and tenderness. You can set standards, maintain discipline, and raise them by the mercy of Jesus. They don't have to play the sports you wanted to play or choose your career path. They can follow the callings of their hearts. They can disappoint you and not bear the scars of your pride and your pain. They can grow up to be vibrant, independent-thinking, loving adults because they did not have to be your Savior.

When we hold our cup out to Jesus, our possessions take their rightful position; they just don't matter as much anymore. I call my children the "Can-I-haves?" I'll tell Paul that I want to go to the grocery store by myself because I don't want to take the "Can-I-haves?" I hate to admit it, but I had pushed past my children and become a full-blown "Gottahave" with God. Gotta have a bigger van, a bigger house, more yard, new clothes, gotta have … gotta have … gotta have. But when my spiritual cup is being filled by my Savior, then I can see the madness of "Gotta have."

Have you ever obsessed about something—let's say, a piano? You spend months pricing and looking, dreaming about where it would go, and finally saving and charging enough to get it. Then, about two weeks after it has been delivered to your house, you find yourself quietly admitting, "We probably didn't really have to have that." When you don't expect things to fill you up, then a new piece of furniture becomes a blessing, not a "Gotta have." We can hold onto our belongings with open hands, allowing the Lord to move His gifts in and out of our lives.

I have told you my full-cup story, but the rest of the story is that I am still tempted. I still catch myself holding my cup out to a girlfriend or to new bedroom furniture, expecting them to fill something that is deeper. The difference is that now I can sense the Holy Spirit prompting me, and I pray from my heart, "Jesus is the answer, not this thing or this person." The wonder of His faithfulness is that God comes and rescues me over and over again. He promises to do the same for you.

God's Promises

The writer of Psalm 73 penned the truth of the full cup long ago. He wrote for us in verses 25-26:

Whom have I in heaven but you?
And earth has nothing I desire besides you.
My flesh and my heart may fail,
but God is the strength of my heart
and my portion forever.

Earlier in this psalm, the writer tells us that he had almost lost his spiritual footing and slipped because he envied the arrogant and the prosperity of the wicked. He looked around and saw the "fullness" of their lives, their good health, position, and wealth. He was tempted to hold out his cup to be filled by their world. But then, in verse 17, he says, "I entered the sanctuary of God; then I understood their final destiny."

What a beautiful picture of our relationship with the Father. He says, "I entered the sanctuary of God." He drew near to God, entering the place where God was and meeting with Him in quietness and intimacy. Understanding and eternal perspective came from being in the presence of the Lord. God graciously showed to him that the ways of the wicked lead to emptiness, ruin, and death.

The Lord filled his cup with an outpouring of understanding and peace. God gave respite to his grieving heart and healed his bitter spirit. The tender mercy of God reminded him afresh that nothing else besides God could fill his desperate soul.

In Psalm 23, the shepherd boy, David, guides us through the magnificent promises of God.

The LORD is my shepherd, I shall not be in want.
He makes me lie down in green pastures,

he leads me beside quiet waters,
he restores my soul.
He guides me in paths of righteousness for his
    name's sake.
Even though I walk through the valley
    of the shadow of death,
I will fear no evil, for you are with me; your rod
    and your staff,
they comfort me.
You prepare a table before me in the presence of
    my enemies.
You anoint my head with oil; my cup overflows.
Surely goodness and love will follow me all the
    days of my life,
and I will dwell in the house of the LORD forever.

Our blessed Shepherd promises to care for every need, providing for our physical bodies, attending to our weariness, and giving comfort to our pain. He will walk with us through every trial that this world may present. He promises to minister to our spirit, restoring and filling until the cup of our soul overflows. He isn't just all that we have; He is more than enough. He is fullness 'til overflowing. He is abundance, blessing, and bounty.

In John 10, Jesus calls Himself the Good Shepherd. His listeners then were much like us and had probably memorized the promises of Psalm 23 as soon as they could walk and speak. Jesus tells us that He is the Shepherd we read about in the Psalms, the one who has come for us, the one who will care for us, our protector and provider. In verse 10, Jesus declares, "I [the Good Shepherd] have come that they may have life, and have it to the full." I especially like the translation Dr. Howard Hendricks would give in our Bible class: "I have come that you may have life, and I mean *really* live!"

Being filled by Jesus doesn't mean a cup full of bland and somber, although some would love to convince you otherwise. Drawing near to the Good Shepherd means that we begin to live as daughters of His glory. Instead of being observers, we get to wake up to our lives and participate. In Jesus, we don't have to be numb just to survive. We can welcome our lives, appreciate the variety, and savor the moments that fill our days.

Our dear Father wants us to know the great fun and blessings of motherhood. He wants us to really enjoy living from the strength of His fullness. He will come, not as a little drizzle, mind you, but like a torrential downpour, sweeping us up into His arms of refuge and pleasure. He wants us to delight in the truth of John 10:10:

I have come so you can really live.

From these and many other promises from Scripture, we can know with assurance that the only person who can fill our souls is our tender and compassionate God. Not only will He fill us, He will fill us to overflowing. And then He promises that to abide with Him, to be filled by His presence and power, will be more than good—those who live in surrender to Him will live in the great joy and blessing of His affection.

Longing for Heaven

Before I leave this chapter on being filled by Christ, I must talk to you about longings. My friend Nicole and I have spent many hours talking about the Lord, and we have wrestled this question to the ground over and over again. But every discussion we have about heaven always begins on the foundation of two truths. The first is Philippians 3:20: "But our *citizenship is in heaven.* And we eagerly await a Savior from there, the Lord Jesus Christ" (emphasis added).

The second truth is found in 2 Corinthians 5:1-5:

> Now we know that if the earthly tent we live in is destroyed, we have a building from God, an eternal house in heaven, not built by human hands. Meanwhile we *groan, longing to be clothed with our heavenly dwelling,* because when we are clothed, we will not be found naked. For while we are in this tent, we groan and are burdened, because we do not wish to be unclothed but to be clothed with our heavenly dwelling, so that what is mortal may be swallowed up by life. Now it is God who has made us for this very purpose and has given us the Spirit as a deposit, guaranteeing what is to come. (emphasis added)

The awesome truth about being adopted by Christ is that we now belong to heaven and our souls long to be there. We hunger for the unity and perfect peace that will not be ours until eternity. We long for the end of suffering. We groan in our spirits to be completely sanctified and wholly devoted to our Savior. We yearn for flawless relationships, model marriages, and infallible parenting. Our hearts ache for heaven.

This is the truth that we must grasp. While we are here, in this earthly dwelling, our Jesus will faithfully come and fill us with His Spirit. He will grant blessing and favor, comfort

There is a widespread belief in the church
that to be a Christian somehow satisfies
our every desire. As one camp song has it,
"I'm inright, outright, upright, downright
happy all day long." What complete non-
sense! Augustine emphasized, "The whole
life of the good Christian is a holy longing. What you desire ardently, as yet you
do not see." So, "let us long because we
are to be filled.... That is our life, to be
exercised by longing."

—JOHN ELDREDGE[1]

and guide, be with us, ever-present and sovereign, and will
protect and provide. But until we stand with Him in eternity,
our souls will long to go home. We will groan in our spirits
and long for that which we cannot have until then.

We are easily deceived and think that all of our longings
can be met on this earth. In fact, our spirit is continually
being refilled until we can be finally filled. One day, in glory,
we shall know the end of wanton desire and debilitating pain.
Our longing will come to an end, and we will be ultimately
and forever full, spending eternity praising God, who set us
apart and brought us home. Our souls will know perfect
peace and rest, our bodies will be healed and glorified, and
our hearts will dance and sing in the presence of the
Almighty.

There are days when I know for sure that the Lord is present and near. I can sense His indwelling and peace, and yet I still ache for more. I have confidently learned to whisper to myself in those moments, "This is my heart longing for home." Sometimes I cry, yearning for what is to come, and sometimes I smile, finding great comfort in remembering that I was made for the glory of heaven.

Motherhood is an incredibly complicated endeavor. It has made us into remarkable women. We can spin plates, juggle balls, sing and dance, and swallow an occasional flaming sword when we have to. We are excellent at getting it all done, at least for a season. But somehow, in the scramble of details and production, we begin to expect that impressive accomplishment will fill our souls. When it doesn't, we turn to the people who are closest to us and desperately charge them with the assignment.

Little by little, over the years, we can unwittingly turn our eyes from our Savior to ourselves, our circumstances, and our families. The changes are subtle, the turning is ever so slight, and years can go by before we recognize that the distance from us to God has become a canyon. When we have not stayed with God, when we do not abide in His presence daily, then we wander recklessly through life, holding our cup out to anyone and anything, doing bigger and better tricks, hoping that one of them, or some mysterious combination of all of them, will fill the empty place.

Our season of motherhood can be radically transformed if we will bring the empty cup of our souls and hold it out to the life-giving water of Jesus. His presence is like a huge cup of java for the soul. His indwelling wakes up our sleepy spirit. To have a soul full of Christ alone is to be overflowing with the water of grace ... soaked through and through by His compassionate love ... sopping wet with the blessings of tender mercy.

But because of his great love for us,

God, who is rich in mercy,

made us alive with Christ

even when we were dead in transgressions—

it is by grace you have been saved.

EPHESIANS 2:4-5

Chapter Four

The Great
Love of God

I never consciously chose to love my children more than I loved God. I never even thought about it very much. They just moved in and took up residence. They completely swept me off my feet, and I tasted a love for them that I had not experienced before—pure devotion for another human being.

Life was new and amazing with children. What am I saying? My life *was* new and amazing, but it was also completely full and exhausting. Somehow in those days, I turned all the affections of my heart toward my family. My spiritual eyes became drowsy and eventually fell fast asleep. I had unwittingly wandered away from the passion and intimacy I had known with God. I began to give as I never had before, and the cup of my soul was drained.

Years passed, and we kept having children. I became more and more involved with my family. Sometime around my

30th birthday, I spent some time taking inventory of my spiritual life, and I was grieved that I had not been growing spiritually. I asked myself:

• Do I love the things that Jesus loves?
• Do I respond in ways that He would respond?
• Do I hunger for Him?
• Do I look more like Jesus this year than I did last year?
• Do I know more of Him?

In some ways, the answers were yes; my heart was tender toward the Lord and His will for my life. But the grim truth was that I wasn't a deeper person. My fellowship with God was from a distance, having lost the intimacy I had once craved. In fact, a closer inspection revealed that my spiritual life had changed very little over the years and I did not look any more like Jesus than I used to.

Now, I had not abandoned my faith. Few around me knew the emptiness inside me. I was coasting, pretending, and drawing from my stored knowledge and experiences, but I wasn't really tasting anything fresh or new from the Lord. Paul and I faithfully attended church and small groups. I prayed and read my Bible. But there was no passion or profound thirst that drove me to Jesus. Numbed by the hugeness of motherhood and spiritually paralyzed by the blur of the years rushing by, I was not growing deeper with God.

I was deeply distressed by the truth I had uncovered about my spiritual life. It scared me to think that real years had raced past me. The treadmill of life had me running as fast as I could, exerting a lot of energy, but going absolutely nowhere. I was _doing_ so much but _becoming_ so little.

Through this self-examination, I came to see that "being"

a godly woman would give value and purpose to all the "doing" in my life.

Does it matter how organized your home is if you do not walk with Jesus? I have come to believe that it does not.

Do well-dressed kids, neatly made beds, and freshly ironed shirts matter? No, not if I sacrifice my soul to make them so.

Does PTA, dinner at six, or a weeded flower bed matter? No.

Please read between the lines here. Being an amazing mommy is fabulous, commendable, a worthwhile goal, but *only* if you have a passionate relationship with God. With all my heart, I can tell you that hardly any of the good things that I "do" really matter if I am not walking with Jesus.

I am not exactly sure how it finally happened. Holding a cup of water at the sink was part of the process. Learning about eyes to see quickened my spirit. But other than that, I don't know if I read something that made a difference. I don't know if someone said something that unlocked my heart. All I know is that I had been asleep and the Lord woke me up.

He gave me new eyes to see what I had been missing, and in my spirit He challenged me to get back to the pursuit of holiness. He ran to me from the distance that I had put between us. And somehow, above the roar of our family and careers, I heard the still, small voice of God calling me to fall in love with Him again.

That calling burned into my soul and I began to pray, "Lord, make me so thirsty for You that I cannot ever be quenched. Increase my desire for You. I want to look more and more like You, less and less like me."

And then the hard prayer, "God, do whatever it takes to restore the passion."

I always get nervous when I pray, "Do whatever it takes," but I can tell you that our God is merciful when He answers. When you ask God to make you thirsty, He does. When you beg Him for passion, He lavishes. And when you plead with Him for life change, He transforms.

Maybe your soul has been asleep, tranquilized by the demands of motherhood, and you are just waking up. You may still be rubbing the sleep from your spiritual eyes, not quite sure where to begin. When my soul began to wake up, I realized that the way back to God was through prayer. I began praying intently for refreshment from God, and I encourage you to begin seeking our Father through prayer.

Ask God to restore the passion and joy. Ask Him to make you thirsty for His righteousness and His presence. Tell Him that you want to fall in love again. Do not be fainthearted in praying.

Pray until He comes.

God always, always comes.

The Lavish Love of God

I grew up in a family where "I love you" was spoken as well as lived. My parents said, "I love you," to my brothers and me all of our growing-up days. To this day, no one in my family can hang up the phone without saying, "I love you." A typical conversation might go like this:

"Hello."

"Hey, I'm at the grocery store. What kind of beans did you ask me to get?"

"String beans."

"Okay, no problem, be home in a minute."

"I love you."

"I love you, too. Bye."

The ritual continues in my own family. Our kiddos may lack in a multitude of areas because of our parental shortcomings, but they will never be able to question our love for them. Paul and I tell them countless times every day, "I love you." I imagine those great words only hold a little meaning for them now. But one day, they will be comforted and encouraged to remember our love for them.

Hearing "I love you" over and over was a gift that my parents gave to me. It built a deep foundation of security. When we know for sure that we are loved and completely accepted, there is both strength and rest.

Do you need to hear your Father tell you that He loves you? Read these words from Scripture and rest in the great comfort of His lavish affection. Pray through these passages and let the Spirit of God work in your heart to draw you in.

> I will sing of the LORD's great love forever; with my mouth I will make your faithfulness known through all generations. I will declare that your love stands firm forever, that you established your faithfulness in heaven itself. (Psalm 89:1-2)

> "Though the mountains be shaken and the hills be removed, yet my unfailing love for you will not be shaken nor my covenant of peace be removed," says the LORD, who has compassion on you. (Isaiah 54:10)

> The LORD appeared to us in the past, saying: "I have loved you with an everlasting love; I have drawn you with loving-kindness." (Jeremiah 31:3)

Who shall separate us from the love of Christ? Shall trouble or hardship or persecution or famine or nakedness or danger or sword? ... No, in all these things we are more than conquerors through him who loved us. For I am convinced that neither death nor life, neither angels nor demons, neither the present nor the future, nor any powers, neither height nor depth, nor anything else in all creation, will be able to separate us from the love of God that is in Christ Jesus our Lord. (Romans 8:35, 37-39)

For God so loved the world that he gave his one and only Son, that whoever believes in him shall not perish but have eternal life. (John 3:16)

Nothing ever changes with God—His love for you, His heart of compassion, His acceptance of you. Just as a mother longs to hold her newborn baby, our dear Father longs to hold you close again. Ask Him to pick you up and carry you back into fellowship. He does not hold a grudge because you have been away for so long. He pursues you so that He can care for you again. You are His daughter, and His love for you is extravagant and pure.

If you have believed that spiritual maturity is only about you, do not be misled—the God who created you will never,

---

This is the most shocking truth of all: The God who knows us truly, loves us still.

BRYAN CHAPELL[1]

ever give up on you. He loves you too much to let you go. You can never outrun the great love of God.

The Mommy Is Still His Child

A few years back, some women asked me to speak to them about our identity in Christ. I agreed, and then realized that I knew very little about my identity in Christ. I began preparing for that conference by listing who and what I am because of Jesus. I continue to add to it as the Lord does new work in my heart and life. I share it with you in hopes that you will be inspired to write your own. Because of Jesus Christ, we are:

the creation of a sovereign God
the beloved who are becoming
saved sinners
forgiven fools
washed in the blood
covered by the cross
esteemed and adored
redeemed and atoned
citizens of heaven
members of the body
adopted orphans
daughters of the King
heirs of great wealth
delivered disciples
recovering Pharisees
lavished in grace
called to be holy
temples of the Spirit
a beautiful fragrance

bond servants
colaborers
set apart for eternity
on our way home

Do you know who you are because of the unfailing, redeeming pursuit of the love of Jesus? Take some time to re-read my list, even writing out to the side who you are because of Him.

Because of the love of Christ, ordinary, sinful, finite women like you and me are being transformed into the likeness of Jesus. Our identity comes from the mighty indwelling work of Christ in us.

Romans 8:29 says that our identity is being "conformed to the likeness of his Son." We are a work in progress because of His love.

There are four parts to this transformation process that God uses in our lives: creation, re-creation, maturity, and consummation.

Stage one: Our creation. You and I have been created in the image of God. No other living creature can lay claim to that truth. The likeness of God is woven through every part of us. Actually, most of our problems spring from losing sight that the very image of God is stamped on us. When God created man and woman in the first chapters of Genesis, He deemed His creation good. He was talking about you, a creation of the Almighty God. He is pleased with His work.

Stage two: Our re-creation. Because we have been marred by our sin, God said, "I will re-create you." Ephesians 2:8-10 reads:

For it is by grace you have been saved, through faith—
and this not from yourselves, it is the gift of God—not

by works, so that no one can boast. For we are God's workmanship, created in Christ Jesus to do good works, which God prepared in advance for us to do.

So how does God re-create? He reshapes us from the inside out. By faith we accept Christ Jesus as our only hope and Savior. He comes, in Spirit, to live in our heart, soul, and mind to do the work of re-creating. By this work of re-creation, God begins to fashion us into His likeness, His workmanship, His treasure, His masterpiece.

And we, who with unveiled faces all reflect the Lord's glory, are being transformed into his likeness with ever-increasing glory, which comes from the Lord, who is the Spirit.

—2 CORINTHIANS 3:18

It is presently about 7:00 P.M., and I am sitting at the public library near my house. The children have been home for the past three days because of snow, and the baby is sick. You now have a clear picture of my mental state.

Paul came home at five this afternoon so that I could get a few hours of writing in before his racquetball game at eight. I have on his sweatshirt, the same sad jeans I have been wearing for a few days, two pairs of socks because it's cold in here, and no makeup or jewelry. I am ashamed to admit it, but I have Milk Duds in my coat pocket that I am secretly eating when the librarian is not looking—my dinner.

I must tell you that I have had a very un-masterpiece-like day. I have felt more like the crumpled-up etching of a frustrated artist, looking as awful as I have felt, heavy heart and restless spirit.

My assignment was to write about our identity in Christ. I realize now that God intended this lesson for me. As I researched and read these passages from my Bible, God reaffirmed that I remain His treasure. In these verses, He has shouted His love for me. Though I came tired and gloomy, God's truth has strengthened my spirit. He proclaims that because I love Jesus—because I have faith in Him—I am still, and always, His masterpiece.

Reading God's Word has revived my soul. What amazing power there is in Scripture! I am sitting at a table all by myself with my laptop and a Bible. Just me, God, and His Word ... and He has ministered to me. Wherever you are, in whatever state of mental or emotional health, may you know the tender mercy of God for your soul—because of your faith in Christ, you have been re-created, you are His treasure: a masterpiece.

Stage three: Maturity—the journey. Remember the Romans 8:29 passage? It tells us that our mission is to conform to the image of God: to look, to talk, and to value like God. The heart of this book is your journey of maturity. Many of us have gotten bogged down in mothering, and we are sitting on hold here. Did you know that God will do whatever it takes, even do what you do not understand, to conform you to His image, to grow you in maturity?

Stage four: Consummation. Read 1 Corinthians 15:51-52:

Listen, I tell you a mystery: We will not all sleep, but we will all be changed—in a flash, in the twinkling of an eye, at the last trumpet. For the trumpet will sound, the dead will be raised imperishable, and we will be changed.

When I read a passage like this, I get excited, sit up a little straighter, and type a little faster. What a fabulous day when our earthly bodies will be changed in an instant, to look like the masterpiece that we are in Christ! The journey will be finished. The reward of heaven and the fellowship of the saints will be ours for all eternity. People like you and me will be the priceless artwork of heaven. Ordinary, normal moms and dads, sons and daughters, who have been transformed—changed into masterpieces by the grace work of God.

Everything That Hinders

William just turned four years old. He is one cute pumpkin, a miniature version of his father. But he can also be incredibly sneaky. One particular afternoon William and my other children had finished their snacks. With my usual presupper instructions, all grazing was officially suspended: "That's it. No more. No sirree, nothing else until dinner. Nada."

"But I'm still hungry."

Sweet smile. Bended knee. Eye to eye. "I'm so glad you're hungry because I am making a great dinner, and you're gonna love it. Hang on, buddy. It won't be long."

I kept working on dinner, distracted by homework and the baby. A little while later, William was trying to walk extra quietly through the kitchen with one hand behind his back. I realized he'd been standing in the pantry.

"Hey, Will, whatcha doing?"

"Nothin'."

"Come here and look at Mommy."

Huge brown eyes turned upward. Solemn face stared blankly. Oreo cookie crumbs fell gently from his lips.

"Whatcha got?"

"Nothin'."

"Are you sure?"

"Yes, ma'am." At four he had already learned the fine art of manners in times of trouble.

"Do you remember what happens when you tell a lie?"

"Yes, ma'am. Big twuble."

"And what happens when you tell the truth?"

"Mur-cee."

"Do you want to tell me the truth? I'll wait."

Silence. Long silence. A four-year-old brain was processing the options. A grimy little hand slowly emerged revealing two Oreo cookies.

"Thank you, Will. Because you told me the truth, you won't get a spanking, but you still have to stand in the corner because you disobeyed Mommy."

"That's mur-cee?"

"Yes, sweetie, that's mercy."

My four-year-old will hide things behind his back and then lie, not understanding how I know. When we are in the middle of a one-handed moment, life cannot proceed until the truth is told and the object is revealed. I blame his sin nature for his hiding and lying, and because we are so easily entangled by our sin, we do the same thing with God.

We hide the dark places of our lives behind our backs, as if God doesn't know or can't see. And yet He is the perfect parent who knows us and loves us enough to put life on hold until we bring what we are hiding into the light, emptying our hands, so that we can receive His tender mercy.

As you begin to wake up to the call of God ... as you begin to thirst for His presence and passion ... as you begin to fall in love again, the Lord will draw you in and hold you close. And yet there is the problem of our sin: It stands between us and God like the glass between a prisoner and his dad, who loves his son but cannot hold him close. The holiness of God cannot have fellowship with the sin and dark places in our lives.

So that you can know Him more deeply, our Father will tenderly begin revealing what hinders your fellowship with Him, asking you to disclose what is behind your back. And then He will wait for the crumbs of truth to fall quietly around you. When you know for sure that the Lord is dealing with you personally about something, you can either think about it for the next five to 10 years, wallow in all the issues, and remain in your pain, *or* you can do whatever it takes to get spiritually healthy.

Life cannot proceed until you bring what is hidden into the light. You and I will not grow in maturity until we open

Who is a God like you, who pardons sin
and forgives the transgression of the rem-
nant of his inheritance? You do not stay
angry forever but delight to show mercy.
You will again have compassion on us; you
will tread our sins underfoot and hurl all
our iniquities into the depths of the sea.

—MICAH 7:18-20

our hands before the Father and give Him the hindrance we have been holding. The choice is yours. You can weigh the options, but when God highlights the hindrance, the healthy response is always obedience. His tender mercy waits for us on the other side of a one-handed moment.

I can type those words so easily, but to live that response is the hinge upon which our entire spiritual life turns. Obedience to the clear leading of God, repenting of sin, turning away from unhealthy choices and relationships, choosing His ways over the world's enticements—these are the places where intimacy is won or lost. We cannot know more of God, trust Him more fully, or hear from Him clearly with the hindrance of our sin between us.

Look at Hebrews 12:1: "Let us throw off everything that hinders and the sin that so easily entangles, and let us run with perseverance the race marked out for us."

To "throw off," means that an action is required. When you are confronted with your unhealthy encumbrance—a one-handed moment—ask the Lord what action He seeks.

Here are some examples of one-handed living that can hinder our love relationship. (But God is so much more creative than I. He will speak to you about the truth of your life.)

- Depression can barge into our lives for any number of reasons. It may require competent counseling and a commitment of time and energies to overcome.

- Dealing with victimization as a young girl and on into adulthood can paralyze the heart and soul. Healing and restoration may mean finding a safe place for honesty and counseling.

- The past and its choices hold on to many women; abortion, addictions, and promiscuity are examples. Again, a safe place or a safe person of refuge and counseling may be the means to repentance and forgiveness.

- A difficult marriage can be a huge hindrance in the spiritual life. The only way to healing may require walking directly through the pain of heartache and disappointment. Choosing to get healthy might mean some very hard conversations and some very real steps toward unity.

- Is there an attraction to another man? Or maybe the distraction of an "image" in your mind ... someone without a face who knows you and loves you perfectly? What about envy and jealousy? The power of dark thoughts stunt spiritual growth, but they lose their power when we bring them into the light and confess them to God.

- We can wrestle under the weight of "Supermomitis." It's a communicable disease easily transmitted in the presence of other Supermoms. There are a couple of antidotes—a whack on the head with a big "Stop trying so hard" stick, or the sweet salve of grace, applied directly to the soul.

- Access to our heart. Who goes there? Who gives advice? Who speaks truth into our lives? Sometimes we are called to distance ourselves from those who drain our souls, run away from those who distract us from Christ.

- Sin is a snare ... the entangler ... the deceiver. Drastic measures may be required in order to flee. A healthy soul is paramount. Fight to be free.

I am only giving some illustrations to get you thinking. The Holy Spirit will speak to you personally about anything that you have hidden behind your back and show you the places that keep you from passion. He will speak to you in the gut of your soul and say, "This has to go so that you can look more like Jesus."

Listen to His gentle leading. He is compassionate. He knows what pain you must walk through in order to be healed. He is merciful and loving. Believe what He promises in Isaiah 44:22: "I have swept away your offenses like a cloud, your sins like the morning mist. Return to me, for I have redeemed you."

I cannot type it loudly enough: Do whatever it takes to *throw off everything that hinders.*

You can trust our God to be with your every baby step. He sees every private struggle and promises to rescue those who call on His name. Return to God. Tender mercy waits for you there.

God Is Bigger

There are women in my life who are not spiritually healthy. They know they are not; we have talked about it, around it, and through it. We have talked until we are all tired of the conversation.

For years, these women have chosen to wallow in the pain and sin of their lives. I have told them of God's love, given them books, prayed, read Scripture, sent letters, and made countless phone calls. But I cannot choose for any of them. From sheer frustration, I have learned that I cannot rush in and save the day. I cannot break through the walls and rescue my friends from the madness of emotional and spiritual death. Believe me, I have tried and failed miserably. Only Jesus is able.

Because of my love for these women, I keep trying to take them to our almighty God. But they will continue to live under the weight of their heavy lives until they choose to accept His love and the freedom it brings. I have listened to them call on His name and then pull back, afraid to fully trust that through the unknown, our faithful God will take care of them. They have to choose to trust Him. I cannot have faith enough for both of us.

It is easier to be friends with Jesus' friends than be friends with Jesus.

—JILL BRISCOE[2]

To "throw off" the encumbrances that hinder our lives and spiritual health means that we have to trust God more than we trust the mess. For some women, there is comfort in the mess, knowing the routine, the words, and the emotions. The mess may be ugly, but they have grown accustomed to looking at it.

If you are spiritually unhealthy, for any number of reasons or circumstances that can make you so, it is urgent that you move toward spiritual healing as quickly as possible. You must do whatever it takes, covered by the grace of God, to get to a healthy place.

It may take years to get healthy, but if you continue to delay, it will only take longer. Otherwise, you waste your life under the mound of encumbrance and never really get to run the race that God has set for you or enjoy the life that He has for you. You will never taste the fullness of His glory and His blessings on earth.

My daddy says, "God never promised us that we wouldn't have to walk through pain. He just said that He would be with us." Praise God, He *is* with us, and He *will* carry you through every difficult place, so that you may come into the blessing of healing.

Regardless of your situation or place, by the power of Jesus, you can have a healthy soul. There may be a process involved. You may have to walk through a lot of pain to get to the glory, but our God will be faithful.

Listening to one's heart and following its promptings can be a stumbling place for many of us. We want to walk with God, but we just keep putting it off. We make pseudo-sanctified to-do lists to be completed before we can have a relationship with God again.

Magic views of Scripture that offer quick solutions for the deep trials of the soul and the great battles of the heart simply do not take sin or Scripture seriously enough.... The Word can conquer sin in a moment, but it may require a season, or a lifetime, or generations.

—Bryan Chapell[3]

Take my advice. Throw away the list and run to Jesus. There is more peace in Him than in a thousand lists of accomplishments. Some of us keep waiting for just the right time to restructure our lives around God. Trust me, there will never be a more right time than this very minute. Do not hesitate any longer and let another year escape. If your heart is being tugged by the thought of falling in love with Jesus again, that is the Holy Spirit.

Just come, my friend, come to Jesus. When you come to Jesus, it means that you turn:

> the affection of your heart,
>> the attention of your mind, and
>>> the intent of your daily life toward Him.

It means that you begin to make conscious efforts to care for your soul by giving God His rightful place in your life. This call to soul care can require a sacrifice of your time and some of your energies. But the blessing of soul care is that, in time, you will fall in love again. Being in love with Jesus is the most powerful and peaceful place I know.

Show me your ways, O LORD,

teach me your paths; guide me in

your truth and teach me,

for you are God my Savior,

and my hope is in you all day long.

Remember, O LORD,

your great mercy and love.

PSALM 25:4-6A

Chapter Five

Soul Care

*I*f you want to make a mom feel guilty, all you have to say is "quiet time." Well, you could also say, "made from scratch," "spray starch," or "handmade," but "quiet time" always gets right to the core of my guilt. At this point in the book, I wish that you and I could be sitting beside each other, talking and interacting, instead of writing and reading. Because if I were with you now, I'd look into your face and tell you truthfully that the practice of caring for my soul is my greatest struggle.

I would quietly ask you the questions I have asked myself:

- Do you sense that the Lord is drawing you closer?
- Do you long for spiritual eyes to see?
- What keeps you from surrendering the cup of your soul for His filling?
- Are you ready to fall in love again?

There is no way around it, I have to spend time with my Father in order to know Him and be filled by His presence. Before children, quiet time used to be an hour or more that I would spend with God, praying, reading, and journaling, a sacred place carved into my day for my Savior.

Now everything has changed. I laugh aloud at the understatement. I am no longer the sweet college coed with Bible studies and FCA meetings, no longer the seminary student who devoted every waking minute to studying the precious Word of God, no longer the starry-eyed young bride who couldn't wait to pray and read the Bible with my husband. I am now the mom of four amazingly energetic, inquisitive, and engaging people. And I love it. I love being a mom. I feel as though my life finally started when they showed up. But how does a mother care for her family *and* care for her soul?

To recollect yourself is to recover all your scattered energies—those of the mind, the heart and the body. It is to reassemble all the pieces of yourself flung in the four corners of your past or the mists of your future, pieces clinging to the fringes of our desires.

—MICHAEL QUOIST[1]

I desire the fullness, peace, and rest of God in my life. But soul care is hard. There have been times in these years of children when it almost seemed impossible to get to a quiet place with God. There have been seasons of forgetfulness, years that I lived in my own strength and frailty, forgetting who I am because of Christ, acting more like a wayward orphan than a daughter of the King.

In his book *Restoring Your Spiritual Passion,* Gordon MacDonald recounts a story told by Mrs. Lettie Cowman:

> In the deep jungles of Africa, a traveler was making a long trek. Coolies had been engaged from a tribe to carry the loads. The first day they marched rapidly and went far. The traveler had high hopes of a speedy journey. But the second morning these jungle tribesmen refused to move. For some strange reason they just sat and rested. On inquiry as to the reason for this strange behavior, the traveler was informed that they had gone too fast the first day, and that they were now waiting for their souls to catch up with their bodies.[2]

Many days I feel like one of those jungle tribesmen: carrying a heavy load, rushing everywhere, cramming more into one day than God ever intended. But the coolie men knew that they had to stop and restore the balance. Too often, I do not.

As long as we keep up the same pace, allowing our bodies to outrun our souls, then we shall remain completely and terminally overcome. The cup of my soul cannot be filled, the longings of my heart cannot be satisfied, and the journey of maturity will never be realized apart from a commitment to spend time with the keeper of my soul, a commitment to soul care.

The Sweet Disciplines of Our Faith

I have heard women say, "If you will spend time with God in the morning, then He will multiply that time and give it back to you in the rest of your day." In reply to that pious adage of false hope, I say, "It just ain't so." As a mom with regular mom responsibilities, any time I give to Jesus in my day is a sacrifice that doesn't necessarily get multiplied and given back to me that day. The multiplication happens in my soul, but the minutes are gone. There is always, and I means always, something else that I could be doing for my family, my work, or our home.

There is an art of leaving things undone so that the greater thing can be done.

—JILL BRISCOE[3]

By the real grace of Jesus, I came to understand that God knows my life. He knows the demands of "be fruitful and multiply." He knows the energy level it takes to care for a family and manage a home. He sees the laundry and the lunchboxes. He oversees homework and goes to basketball games. He is not frustrated by my commitment to care for the ones He has entrusted to me. He is not angry that I am up all night with a new baby or a sick child and too exhausted to read my Bible. He understands our season completely, and I know that He gives grace to mothers in abundance.

And yet—there is no way around it—even though I live in the blessing of His generous grace, I must spend time with my Father. The disciplines of our faith are the means by which we walk in intimacy. I cannot know the Father by osmosis, and believe me, there were years that I tried. A Bible on my night table does not miraculously transfer into my heart and mind while I sleep. Listening to someone else pray does not necessarily mean that I am praying. I have listened to other people pray and, because of my weariness, never engaged my heart or agreed with them in my mind. They prayed, but I did not.

Becoming thirsty for God renewed my commitment to spiritual disciplines. I was also inspired and challenged by the story of Susanna Wesley, the mother of John and Charles, two great men in the history of our faith. In the early 1700s she gave birth to 19 children. Four died at birth and five more of her children died later. Story has it that in order to spend time with God, Susanna would sit in the corner and put her apron over her head. No one was allowed to speak to her when she was underneath the apron because that was her time with God. I laugh every time I think about that picture, and yet I am inspired by her creativity and perseverance. Can you hear the children whispering, "Shhh, don't speak to mother, she's underneath the apron"?

I decided that if I was going to grow spiritually, I had to get creative. My old patterns with God were not working anymore. I needed to wake up to my new life of motherhood and become more resourceful about my time with the Lord. These pages are my testimony, my spiritual work in progress. I share with you from my struggles and from the victories.

Before we titled this book, I half-jokingly called it "How to Be a Mama and Still Love God." All of my mom friends would laugh when I told them the working title and then seriously add, "I really need that book." I have met a few moms who haven't been spiritually sidetracked by motherhood, but most of the women I know are a lot like me—they have struggled to maintain a tender walk with Jesus.

Since waking up to the beauty and power of my Savior, I am choosing to live, as much as it is possible, an intentional life. I don't want life to just happen to me; instead, I want my walk with the Lord to affect the way that I live and grow. I want to integrate the disciplines of faith into my life. A healthy soul and a pure life don't just happen, no more than I will wake up one day and have a great marriage or a fulfilling purpose in my life. It all requires deliberate pursuit.

To be sleep-deprived is better than being God-deprived.

—JILL BRISCOE[4]

I was at a women's retreat recently with the assignment of leading a small group, made up of moms like me with similar-aged children. There were about 10 of us, and at the end of our weekend, we put away the discussion guides and I asked the women to tell me how they cared for their souls.

Blank stares.

I rephrased the question, "How do you actually get time with God? How do you remain sane and spiritual in these years?"

More blank stares and lots of quiet.

Finally one woman said boldly, "I pray in the shower every morning. Boy, I really couldn't make it through the day if I didn't have that time with God."

"Okay … good … anybody else?" I asked.

Another woman chimed in, "I put on a worship tape and turn it up loud when I am cleaning the house."

A few other women joined in, "Yep, that's what I do too. It just makes the work go so much faster when I'm singing to the Lord."

I politely smiled and listened while my heart broke. We were called to dinner before I could say, "There is more. We can have more intimacy than shower prayers and vacuum praise … there is more."

In these pages, I want to put some handles on the theory of intimacy. Let's look at several areas of spiritual discipline and see how a growing relationship with God can really happen in these years of mothering. I am going to tell you how I spend time with God, but only for the sake of inspiration and to spark your creativity. How you spend time with God will look entirely different, but maybe something I say will motivate you toward creativity and consistent pursuit. What I hope to give to you is a fresh commitment to the disciplines of our faith, tenderized by the mercy of Jesus, covered with the grace He so freely gives.

Everything to God in Prayer

I am completely convinced that there is no power in our lives because we do not pray. As a mom, I thought that I had been faithful to pray, and I had. But my prayers were not intimate prayers, they were "McPrayers," said on the go, in a moment of need, and in places of convenience. In these last years, I have become committed to "real prayer," taking every joy, praise, concern, and worry to God. And my life is different because of the power and peace that come from the discipline of praying. I respond differently. My spirit rests. My heart is not anxious.

The angel fetched Peter out of the prison. Prayer fetched the angel.

—SEEN ON A CHURCH SIGN

For me, praying is intentionally putting myself in the presence of God. Hear these prayer instructions from the powerful Word of God:

> Therefore I tell you, whatever you ask in prayer, believe that you have received it, and it will be yours. And when you stand praying, if you hold anything against anyone, forgive him, so that your Father in heaven may forgive you your sins. (Mark 11:24-25)

> Do not be anxious about anything, but in everything, by prayer and petition, with thanksgiving, present your requests to God. And the peace of God, which transcends all understanding, will guard your hearts and your minds in Christ Jesus. (Philippians 4:6-7)

> Pray for those who mistreat you. (Luke 6:28)

> Be joyful always; pray continually; give thanks in all circumstances, for this is God's will for you in Christ Jesus. (1 Thessalonians 5:16-18)

> Is any one of you in trouble? He should pray. Is anyone happy? Let him sing songs of praise....The prayer of a righteous man is powerful and effective. (James 5:13, 16b)

To intentionally get into the presence of God in this season of mothering can be quite a feat, but it can be done. With a little creativity and persistence, we can know sweet communion with God.

In the Presence of God

"Just five more minutes" has taken on a whole new meaning for me. I try not to get out of bed in the morning without Jesus. I have to thank Paul for the inspiration. When his clock goes off, he rolls over and hits the snooze, and with his face in his pillow, he prays until he gets up. From him, I have learned the blessing of praying for those five more minutes before my clock goes off again.

The only thing consistent about my prayer life in the rest of my day is that I am always looking for a time to pray. I used to think that the house had to be quiet and the children had to be napping before I could pray, but I have learned differently. When Grayson was a baby, I would put him in the swing and lie on my face in front of him to pray. Now that

We make prayer the preparation for work; it is never that in the Bible. Prayer is the exercise of drawing on the grace of God. Don't say, "I will endure this until I can get away and pray." Pray now; draw on the grace of God in the moment of need.

—OSWALD CHAMBERS[5]

our baby days are over, I can still get away to my room for a quiet time of prayer during a video or some game they are playing. I go into my room and leave the door open so that I can hear if there is a catastrophe and so they can find me.

For some reason I used to worry about being interrupted while I was praying, but I don't worry anymore. The picture of their mommy praying is one that I want my children to have. Now, if the children find me praying, they are more likely to come and kneel down beside me than to interrupt. They may not stay beside me long, but they have come to realize that praying is reverent and quiet. I will hear them in the hall saying to one another, "Mommy is praying."

I know it does not make one a more proficient pray-er, but for me, it has become important to pray on my face before the Lord at some point during the day. Just the act of lying prostrate on the floor before my Father humbles my heart and gives great clarity to my thoughts and attitude toward God. It is very hard to be prideful and arrogant when my face is smashed into the carpeting. Little kids may come and climb on your back and try to work their little face up into yours, but love them and pray on. Again, what a blessing you give them when they see you pray. William asked me recently, "Why were you sleeping on the floor?"

"I was praying, honey."

"Oh, it looked like sleeping."

Smile. It has been known to happen.

Writing is a great way to stay focused on the intent of your prayers, so we will spend time on journaling in the next chapter. Many times I write my prayers in my journal. Another friend, Bonnie Bonnette, journals her prayers on her computer. When she tells me, "I'll pray for you," she writes the most beautiful, inspiring prayers and e-mails them to me. I have saved every prayer she has sent to me so I can go back and pray them again.

I am very rarely in my minivan alone, but when I realize that it is just me, I turn off the radio and pray aloud, which keeps me praying while I am driving. It also keeps me mindful that I really am a pitiful pray-er. When I pray aloud by myself, I hear myself stumbling, uhhh-ing, and rambling, and I am motivated to improve—to bless God, not bore Him.

When we thirst for God, we want to pray. We begin to crave the intimacy and the fellowship. While there is nothing wrong with praying in the shower or in your car, try to pursue a quiet place and time to pray. I really do pray in my closet, kneeling beside the shoe boxes, because it is quiet and empty of distraction. Can you find a place of sanctuary for quiet and reverent prayer? Can you take this one discipline and cultivate consistency? A mother must find creative ways to get into the presence of God.

"God isn't interested in a bunch of yarping." I can still hear Albert Long teaching from the front of a crowded room in the student union. At the University of North Carolina, I attended FCA on Thursday nights, and Albert Long would speak to us every few months. Mr. Long was one of only a few men to letter in four sports at Carolina. When he was going to speak, I had to get to FCA early because the room would be packed. Everyone knew they were going to hear from a passionate man who walked with Jesus. Through the years, Mr. Long gave us an acrostic for praying that I use to this day. It goes something like this:

P - Praise - In the first part of your prayer, give praise and adoration to God.

R - Repent - Then repent of your sin and anything that stands between you and the Lord.

A - Ask - Ask anything for anybody. This is a time for intercession.

Y - Yourself - Ask for yourself.

He would always finish with, "Remember to P-R-A-Y, that's pray. Backwards it spells Y-A-R-P, yarp, and that's not what God asks us to do." How poignant that lesson has been for me. Albert Long gave order to my prayers. I am still learning to P-R-A-Y instead of yarp.

When a Mother Prays

A few years ago I met a now-dear friend, Katie Garrett. Katie is one of the four children of Barry and Carol St. Clair. Paul and I worked with the St. Clairs at many conferences, and I had taken pages of notes at several parenting seminars they taught. I was always drawn to Carol because of her vulnerability and gracious spirit, and though I didn't really know her, I vividly remember her smile. A godly mom and mentor who lived an intentional life, Carol taught her children about the faithfulness of God and the power of prayer. Sadly, Carol died not long ago at the young age of 52.

When I met Carol's daughter, Katie, she was 22 and had just lost her mom. She had graduated from Furman University in May, gotten married in June, moved with her new husband to Orlando, Florida, to begin seminary in July, and lost her precious mother in August. At her tender age, Katie had just undergone more life changes than many of us face in 20 years. Katie and her husband, Bart, moved into a cute little house only a few miles from us, and God moved Katie into my heart.

You know, all those parenting seminars don't really mean anything until you meet the children of the teachers. And when I met Katie St. Clair Garrett, I searched long and hard until I found those notes I had taken. Her parents did something right, and I wanted to remember what they had said. I don't think that I have ever met a young woman who has captured my heart so fiercely with her deep and mature passion for God. I walked with her during those agonizing months after her mom died, and she modeled for me the grace and goodness of God.

I met with her almost every week while we lived in Florida, and after only a few weeks, I began to ask God to give me tender, valiant daughters like Katie Garrett. Because I had fallen in love with Katie, I wanted to know the mom who had poured into her life. I would ask Katie all kinds of parenting questions, "What were your rules about bedtime and homework? When did you have to be home? How did your mom deal with attitudes and bickering?" I had only known Katie's mom from a distance and notes on a page, but through Katie, I got to know the heart and passion of Carol.

I asked Katie to tell me about her mother and prayer:

My "mommie," Carol, would combine the art of journaling with her prayer time. Being a busy mother of four, she would steal away time whenever it allowed. In the morning, she would sit at the kitchen table after carpool. In the afternoon, she would find a place of solitude while we played or finished our homework. In the evening, after she loved on us and tucked us into bed, she treasured a few more quiet moments to reflect on the day and evaluate her thoughts.

By writing out her prayers to God, she could "rehash" her constant joy, struggles, requests, temptations, as well as God's repeated faithfulness. Since my mommie passed away almost two years ago, I am now the proud owner of her prize possessions, her journals.

As I read back through her writings, I saw the various seasons of her life. There were many voices: cries of healing, shouts of joy, pleading for healing, begging for forgiveness, asking for understanding, thanksgiving for specific answers, unanswered questions, but most often rejoicing for specific ways that God had been faithful. Her journals were a great outlet for those thoughts and emotions. The freedom to write gave her the freedom to open her heart before God. She would often read back through past entries and recount how God's hand had moved. What a tangible way to know God better.

My mother spent the majority of her time loving and serving us. Therefore, her "praying life" was focused on her family. She learned to pray creatively and specifically for her kids. She used bedtime as a point in the day to lay her hands on us and commit our lives to the Lord. She and my daddy modeled prayer in front of us as we knelt by our beds together.

In our school years, she would rally some other moms to pray on a weekly basis for God to work mightily in the lives of our friends. They would walk around the campus claiming it for Christ. My husband has adopted that same idea of prayer walks now in our neighborhood.

Beginning in high school and then on into college, my mom would write out her prayers for me in letter form. She usually claimed a verse or passage of Scripture for a certain season of my life. By writing it down, she reminded me of her love and at the same time, taught me how to pray creatively for my family.

In college I have a specific, vivid mental picture of my relationship with Mom and Dad. I would sit on the floor out in the hall between the doors and the stairs on my portable phone and pour out my ever-changing heart to them. Every time they would listen and cry with me, and then say, "Katie, let us pray for you." It always soothed my soul.

I specifically remember having a paralyzing fear of going back to college one year and feeling overwhelmed. In order to conquer those worries, my mom helped me to see the power of prayer. She asked me to envision banners of God's promises as I drove into the front gates of my college. The banners were claiming the victory I had in Christ. I was having a hard time grasping this concept, so she made these tiny banners out of toothpicks to place at the front gates of Furman, as well as at the end of my bed and in my car. Those creative visuals reminded me of the power in claiming God's Word over my anxieties.

The things my parents did and modeled for me were not magical. However, they made prayer a tangible and desirable act of worship to our Father. It became a part of who we were as a family. I am grateful now to have such a precious view of the intimate act of prayer because I had a mommie and daddy who prayed.

I am inspired by the life of Carol, and by the beautiful testimony of her life in Katie, to be a mother who prays.

Listening to God—a Conversation

For 38 years, Mary Geegh was a missionary to India. In 1970, she wrote a little book called *God Guides,* chronicling the powerful work of God in her ministry. She states at the beginning of her writing:

> When I went to India and started to work in a village, I found many things very wrong. I preached to the people; I prayed for them, but I did all the talking. Sometimes I pleaded with God a whole night for a person to change and turn from the power of Satan to the power of Christ. Nothing seemed to happen.

She goes on to tell of another missionary who came to her village, Dr. L. R. Scudder, who met with a very troubled man from their village. He sat with him while the man poured out his past, and then Dr. Scudder instructed him to be still and wait for the Lord. They sat together and the villager realized how wrongly he had been living. He "listened" to the Holy Spirit and surrendered his life to Christ, obeying Him in everything. All the people saw this man change his ways and were amazed at the power of God in his life. Then they, too, sought the power of God for their lives.

She continues:

> Then the people said to me, "See! You have worked so hard here for over a year, but none of us have changed. Dr. Scudder came here for one week, and

now we are all changed. He taught us how to have the power of the Holy Spirit in our daily lives."

I asked Dr. Scudder, "How do I begin to have the power of the Holy Spirit, to help people?" He told me: "The first step is to wait ... be still ... listen. Then be definite about your sins—daily; with notebook and pencil write down the things the Holy Spirit speaks to your mind; determine to obey. Then share with others who come to you for help how the power of Christ changes you."[6]

The rest of this tiny book is filled with 50 listening stories, evidence of God's powerful guidance in the life and ministry of Mary Geegh. She learned from the visiting missionary the discipline of sitting, with pad and pencil in hand, waiting until she had a clear direction from the Lord.

In the morning she would sit in "listening prayer" and wait until she had a clear thought about how to proceed with her day. Others would come to her with their burdens and they would sit together and listen until there was an answer or directive. Her testimony is filled with miracles, changed lives, and the powerful witness of "listening" for the Holy Spirit. She dedicated her whole life to listening to God and then faithfully obeying His guidance.

As I have learned to incorporate "listening prayer" into my spiritual disciplines, my prayer life has been severely altered. I am hearing with my heart and mind a voice that is not audible but rings in my head, making it seem louder and clearer. Some of the clear thoughts that have come to me have been very ordinary thoughts, but they seem to burn fiercely in my mind when I am listening. They include things like:

Do not turn on the television today.

Call Paul and invite him to lunch.
Go play with AnnaGrace.
At other times I have "heard" more-convicting thoughts like:
Ask Paul for forgiveness.
Stop being selfish … stop thinking about yourself.
Confess your sin aloud to a kindred heart.

It is so much easier to obey the less-convicting directives, but I have found that the Lord won't leave me alone until I follow through and obey, even in the hard places.

"Listening" to God is moving me beyond my sometimes-chatterbox prayer life into real conversation with my Father. I am learning to "hear" what my Father wants me to do.

Someone has said, "If the Father had access to you, He could change the world." Right now in my life, I want the Father to have complete access, but I'm not as interested in changing the world as I am in His changing me. The world may come later, but I'm asking God to use these disciplines of soul care to make me different and better.

In this chapter, we dove into soul care by considering the discipline of prayer, but we're just getting started. There is so much more to intimacy and spiritual health. I'll see you in the next chapter.

Therefore, I urge you, brothers,

in view of God's mercy,

to offer your bodies as living sacrifices,

holy and pleasing to God—this is your

spiritual act of worship. Do not conform

any longer to the pattern of this world,

but be transformed by the renewing

of your mind. Then you will be able

to test and approve what God's will is—

his good, pleasing and perfect will.

ROMANS 12:1-2

Chapter Six

It Is Well with My Soul

*E*very woman who becomes a mother enrolls herself in the graduate-level course of higher sacrifice. Motherhood teaches a woman how to deny herself. When money is tight, the children are clothed and fed first. When energy is low, nighttime books still get read. Mothers give and give, long past exhaustion and reasonableness.

My sister-in-law dragged herself out of bed a few days after delivering her third baby to sit at a sewing machine and make fall festival costumes for her older boys. I have a friend who went in to check on her son long after bedtime. He asked for a brownie in his lunch the next morning, and because she loved him and wanted to bless him, she made brownies around midnight.

Our protective, provider instincts take over as soon as our babies get here and we begin to transfer to the children all the attention that we used to give to our bodies and our souls.

Sacrifice and self-denial are very good things. But when it comes to our souls, we can sacrifice too much. There is a line we can cross, going too far, giving ourselves into spiritual poverty.

Soul care is about replacing what has been given out. This is not aromatherapy or deep-breathing exercises. This is not a facial or an exfoliating body wrap. Although that all sounds wonderful, my body will be pampered but my soul will be left empty. This is about getting into the supernatural presence of God—the place of miracles, the place of filling.

Let's press on; there are more sweet disciplines of our faith.

The Light for My Path

The Bible is the voice of God, spoken directly into our lives. In Psalm 119:105, the writer tells us about the purpose of Scripture: "Your word is a lamp to my feet and a light for my path."

The Scriptures illuminate for us God's will and heart. They shine the light of His leading into the darkness of our unknown. They clear the way so that our feet will not stumble. His words give direction, comfort, and encouragement. Scripture brings the shadows of our sins into the light of day. God's words admonish and rebuke. They act as a beacon, calling us back to the path of righteousness and godliness. The Bible is full of God's promises to cover us with mercy and grace. In this journey toward maturity and Christlikeness, we will remain wanderers in the dark without the powerful Word of God to light our path.

There is truly no end to the relevance and application of the Scriptures. Paul and I want to raise our children according to the precepts of the Bible. We are learning how to manage our money based on scriptural principles, how to be married, how to minister to others, and how to live in this world and in these days. As mothers, you and I must become students of the Word of God. Is it possible that in motherhood we need the Word of God more that at any other time in our lives?

As with all the other disciplines, the difficulty is actually finding time to open your Bible and process the words. One year for Christmas, someone gave me a verse-a-day calendar that I placed in the window over my sink. That year was one of my overwhelming years, with one in preschool and two in diapers. Sometimes the calendar went for days without my having enough energy to even rip off the page. If it had not been for that calendar, I am not sure I would have read very much of God's Word that year. It makes me feel sad even to tell you, but the truth is that this season is plagued with exhaustion and busyness that can rob our spiritual lives.

I remember hearing a story about a mom whose child was

Yesterday's spiritual passion cannot be today's energy. Passion quickly dissipates; it must be restored. Like the manna God gave the Israelites in the desert, spiritual passion spoils quickly. As Moses and his people had to collect manna daily, so must we restore spiritual passion regularly. We would be wise to know how it so quickly disappears and what we can do when that happens.

—Gordon MacDonald[1]

sick. The child had been sick for days, and they were both exhausted. The husband came home one evening to find his wife on the sofa with their sleeping child sprawled across her lap, and propped on the child was the Bible. This exhausted mom had found a moment and chose to give it to God. The husband was humbled by the picture of her faithfulness, and I am always inspired by the story.

I have found that if I am going to get moments or longer in the Word, then it needs to be available. I try to have a Bible everywhere—in the kitchen, in the bathroom, in the living room, by my bed, and in my car. Falling in love again has made me thirsty for the truth of God. My time for reading and study is becoming more and more consistent, but having a Bible close by makes it easier for me.

I wait to eat my breakfast until after the children are fed and settled. Instead of poring over the mail or a catalog, I have been reading from my *One Year Bible* at breakfast. If I don't get finished at breakfast, no problem; I pick it up later at lunch or while I am waiting for dinner to finish. The key is having it close by. If I have to go find it, I may not do it. The same is true of keeping a Bible in my car. Inevitably, several times a week I will end up sitting somewhere and waiting for someone, in a carpool or after a practice. If there is a Bible handy, then I can get a couple of chapters in and even read aloud to the kids in the car.

The Word of God is food for my soul, feeding me in the deeper places. The intensity of my yearning weakens. My frustrations begin to melt. My grievances fade in the light of God's instruction. We have to remind ourselves in the practice of spiritual disciplines that these pursuits feed our souls. I am not reading the Word of God just to check something off my super spiritual to-do list. I am not reading so that I can fill out some questions on a page. My purpose is not greater knowledge or more verses memorized, although there is nothing wrong if those things happen. My purpose is to care for my soul. I am reading so that I may be filled up by the truth of my Savior. I am reading so that my soul will not suffer and acquiesce. I am reading so that I might know more about the One that I want to look like.

Begin any way you must: a verse-a-day calendar, the Bible on tape, a chapter in the morning and a chapter at night. Read through the Gospels. Read the chapter in Proverbs that corresponds with today's date. Get a *One Year Bible.* I don't really care how you begin, but *that* you begin is my plea. My grandmother says, "Things just go better when I read my Bible." Yes, yes they do. Things *do* just go better because there is power in the reading and hearing of God's Word.

Journaling

Over the years, I have begun journaling too many times to recount, with stacks of partially filled notebooks dating back to high school. My head always knew that there was benefit to journaling, but consistency in the discipline seemed to elude me. After college, I remember being particularly inspired to journal by Gordon MacDonald's book *Ordering Your Private World.* Persuaded by Mr. MacDonald's exhortation, I began to journal with greater devotion, yet still with sporadic consistency.

About five years ago at the time of this writing, a friend gave me a beautiful journal with wonderful papers, and somehow the timing was right. I bought a great pen, saved the journal until my next personal retreat, and began to write. I filled up those pages with my ramblings and prayers. I spent days remembering the past few years and recording the events. After laughing and crying over my pages, I came away from that weekend completely committed to the discipline of journaling.

While family events and decisions find their way into the writing, my journal is mostly reserved for me. It is the place where I say and shout the truth of my insecurity and my weakness. It is the place where I dream out loud and beg God for His help and His wisdom. It's where I wrestle with the gap between what is and what could be. In my journal, I can fall to pieces and then watch Him put me back together. I confess my sin, pray toward repentance, and lament my lack of discipline until my Father comes and rescues me. My journal is the

---

A Journal Entry

18 February   *2:30 p.m.*

Friday   *home*

It's the first day of my period, again—freight train day—the day I feel as if I have just been run over and dragged along by the caboose. I am exhausted. Why does life have to be lived in cycles of energy and weakness? Why can't I know a consistently strong body and mind? I am so tired . . . blurry vision and no real competent thoughts . . . overcome by my inadequacy. Oh Jesus, come. Come and hold me tight. I love You. I need Your mercy and grace.

record of my angst and my joy. My journal is a place where I care for my soul.

I have another book in which I write things about the children. Every so often, I write out my impressions about where they are in life, what they are doing, or cute things they have said and done. Sometimes I actually remember to write them a "letter" on their birthday. I don't give them their letters but save them in the book for later. Their stories and letters go into a book that I keep in the drawer beside my bed. My journal is saved for me, and I take it everywhere.

Journaling would not be as powerful for me if Paul and I did not have a privacy rule. He doesn't read my journal. He knows that I don't have anything to hide and he can read it if he ever feels he needs to … but he doesn't. His complete trust (and probably lack of interest in my girly stuff) gives me the freedom to process my life and struggles without judgment. If I thought that my words were going to be read sometime in the next 50 years, I am sure that I would write with greater reserve and hesitation.

Sometimes I write my prayers to God. Some days I make lists so that I can see an issue more clearly. Other days, I explore a verse of Scripture. Sometimes I have written one line to say that I am too exhausted to write. But in the privacy of a journal, through the years of pilgrimage with my faithful God, I have seen my immaturity become greater maturity, my lack of discipline become more discipline, and watched as my soul without dreams became filled to overflowing. But the amazing thing about journaling is that I have come to see the hand of God in my pages.

In the Old Testament, when God answered prayer or rescued the people from suffering, they stopped and built a monument to God so that the people would always remember. My journal is filled with the monuments of my words, testimony to the grace and mercy of God.

I am so thankful that I was journaling around the time that Paul and I dated. Years later, when we were married and having a particularly difficult season, I pulled out my old journal and began to read. I had prayed so hard over the decision to marry Paul, and it was all there on spiral-bound pages in faded blue pen. I had lists of reasons to marry him and lists of reasons why I couldn't marry any of the other men who had been in my life. When Paul asked me to marry him, I was more sure of my response than I had been of any decision I had ever made. That old journal was a monument to God's leading and the rightness of our marriage. Just re-reading those pages was healing for me. I remembered how God had led me, and those words renewed my spirit.

My journals have also been a great monument to the patient hand of God—the library of my immaturity; volumes of evidence of my Father's grace and love for me. It can be embarrassing, but profitable, for me to read through the years and see how the Lord is tenderly growing me up.

I urge you to buy a beautiful journal. Better yet, ask for a journal for your birthday. Then give yourself permission to write the truth of your soul. Watch how the Lord comes to minister to you as you build monuments to His grace and His love in your life.

Solitude

I believe that most of the people who know me would label me an extrovert—someone who gets energy from being with other people. At one level, they would be right. I can get completely caught up in interaction, connecting with and being challenged by others. But there is the deeper part of me that craves solitude. I have concluded that I am really an introvert who pretends to be an extrovert. I love to be with people, but I need the healing balm of quiet and aloneness.

Now, here is my quandary. I am the mother of four children, and I am rarely alone. I do not go the bathroom alone. I do not take a bath without knocks on the door or someone wiggling the doorknob that I have locked. I do not go to bed alone, nor sleep alone, nor wake up alone. I am rarely in the car alone. My whole day is full of people. There are no random moments of solitude.

But Jesus often withdrew to lonely places and prayed.

—LUKE 5:16

And so, I fight for solitude. "Fight" and "solitude" don't seem to go together, but that is how I have to think about it. I must be aggressive, prepared to battle all the obstacles that would keep me from this discipline that nourishes my soul. I have a valise that I keep packed with books, pens, and pads of paper. Whenever a window of quiet opens up, I just throw in my Bible and journal, and I am off.

Sometimes when I am running an errand alone and have some extra time, I will sit in the car for 30 minutes before I go into the store, just being quiet. If I feel led to write or read, then I am prepared. Other times I will stop at the park and sit on the grass for a while. Paul knows how deeply I need alone time, and so some days after work he will say, "You just go out for a while."

Usually, I'll grab my bag and head to the library, where I can sit and be quiet. In all my years of "public library quiet," I have seen very few other mom types. I love it because I can't spend any money. It's low-calorie because they don't let you eat or drink, only sit and be quiet. Actually, I am at the library right this very moment, and the only moms who have been here hurried in and out with their children. Try the library sometime for solitude. If it causes you too much post-college stress to be in the library, find a bookstore with great coffee and comfy chairs.

I actually began walking just for the opportunity to retreat from my family. Some nights, after dinner, I hand bath time over to Paul and hit the sidewalk. My head is usually swirling after a full day of input, and it can take 20 or 30 minutes just to get my head cleared and my heart settled. I have to pray through everybody and their stuff, and organize my thoughts, just so I can get to my own soul. The last 20 minutes of walking are real times of depth, solitude that cares for my soul. I can go back into the house as a peaceful mother.

My friends marvel at the lengths I go to for solitude, but quiet feeds my spirit. I will go on pastors' retreats with Paul and stay in my room for the better part of the day without turning on the TV. Most of the other wives go shopping, but I am in a season of life where I can't buy quiet. So I will sneak out for a solo walk on the beach or sit on my balcony listening to the music of crashing waves.

I like to go to a restaurant by myself with a book. My favorite outing is breakfast at a place around the corner in the winter. I drop the children at Mother's Day Out and then retreat to the warmth of their huge fireplace. I sit in front of it and read until I am toasty and then eat a meal that somebody else prepared. It is heaven to me. I realize how completely weird

I sound, but I am a better wife and a much better mother when I have been alone. I am more fun and much more patient because my soul has been stilled.

Sometimes all the people and talk that fill our world keep us from hearing and seeing the Father. Are there moments carved into your life for solitude? What could you do differently? What arrangements could you make for some precious quiet for your soul?

A Personal Retreat

The times when I have actually gone away for a personal retreat have been quite rare. Sometimes when I am going to a women's retreat or conference, I have been able to get away a half day early for an afternoon of personal retreat before the event, but more often than not, I have my personal retreats at home.

Sometimes a day or a good portion of a day will break free or miraculously appear in my schedule. I recognize the value of a "free day" without any commitments, so I begin to protect that day, quietly planning for myself a personal retreat

I sit on my favorite rock, looking over the brook, to take time away from busy-ness, time to be. I've long since stopped feeling guilty about taking being time; it's something we all need for our spiritual health, and often we don't take enough of it.

—MADELEINE L'ENGLE[2]

at home. If I have to stay in the house, I will work really hard the night before my "retreat" so I will not be distracted. I will make a dent in the laundry, pay the bills, make sure the kitchen is really clean before I go to bed, attending to those things that could steal my day or distract my heart.

The next morning after everyone is gone, I retreat. My first beeline is to the phone. I turn off all the ringers and turn down the answering machine. Depending on the day, I might go for a long walk next, but somewhere in there, I take a bath. It feels so sneaky and indulgent to take a great bath about 10:00 A.M. on a Saturday while everyone is away. I light candles, bring my book, even have a snack if I want to. As my body begins to relax and unwind, my mind transitions from craziness into caring for my soul.

We often enter [our prayer time] ... while we are still emotionally out of breath. It is hard at first to concentrate our thoughts and to bring them into the presence of the Lord. We have to quietly relax for a short season while the mind accustoms itself to spiritual activity.

—GORDON MacDONALD[3]

The next hours of my at-home retreat are spent with Jesus, practicing these disciplines of soul care. It's not quite as dreamy as a retreat by the beach or on top of a mountain, but I'm telling you, it's a great way to spend a day in the presence of God.

Great Thinkers

Every once in a while, we need to be stretched. In the season of mothering, we can lose ourselves in the faraway land of our children's multiplication tables, treat bags for a class of 20, baseball practice, and sleepovers. To their busy little lives, add one generous husband who has asked 50 people over for a fellowship brunch, and before you know it, your family is all you think about.

Based on the ages of our children, this season of busy family is due to last a good 25 to 30 years. In that span of time, I know that my mind will completely turn to dust if I do not feed it with great thinkers and new ideas. To sit under an astute thinker or read a classic work is to care for the beauty of my soul—to care about what I am becoming.

These moments of new instruction are still quite rare for me because my family comes first. But I try to grab them whenever I can. I have friends who don't live in the land of mothering, and I ask them what they are reading. I cannot keep up with them, but I am compiling a reading list of books that I am very slowly working through. I will hear about a great sermon and ask for the tape.

Recently I listened to the 10-tape series from the Moody Pastors' Conference. Not your typical input for mothers, but it was so refreshing to think about something besides what to fix for dinner. I have to admit, it was a stretch to hang on through the academia of John Piper because of all the dust in my brain, but I did, and my mind was strengthened by his words and reasoning.

Maybe you are not interested in literature or lectures. Maybe you are craftsy (I am a craftsy wanna-be), and it would feed your soul to take a one-night cooking class or go to the how-to seminar at Home Depot. Go. I know that we cannot spend a lot of time in this arena, but when you have the opportunity, jump in. Learn something new. Think about something different. Have your mind and abilities stretched and honed. It will feed your soul to learn.

Exercise

There is no denying that your soul is intricately woven with your mind and your body. A good reason so many of us lack the desire to pursue spiritual things is because we are exhausted. We have only so much energy to use in a day, and the tyranny of the urgent takes it all. Our bodies are run down and sluggish. Our minds shut down at the end of the day, begging us to stop processing information and exerting energy.

After four pregnancies, I speak to you from a body that is in process. I am soon to be 38 years old and carrying 20 extra pounds. Nothing about me is toned, except possibly that muscle in my arms that enables me to pick up my children; they are getting heavy. This time last year, I carried 40 extra pounds, and I am on a mission to return to greater health and fitness. Writing a book hasn't done anything to improve my physical health. With every new paragraph to write, I feel a hunger pang. I am being held accountable for my eating and exercise even as I write.

You see, losing weight, beginning to walk, doing sit-ups beside my bed, doing girl push-ups until I could do one boy push-up—these improvements have made a difference in my body and in my mind. I feel myself waking up, and my soul is reaping the benefits of a stronger me. I am caring for my soul through the discipline of exercise.

Believe me, I know how difficult it is to begin. But can you begin somewhere? I began by walking 10 minutes away from my house and then turning around to walk the 10 minutes back. Pretty soon, I wanted to walk 12, and so on. I started with five girl push-ups, but then one day I could do 10. Where can you begin with the discipline of exercise? A revived body will soon give strength to your weary soul.

The Fruit of Discipline

"Do you really think it matters if I grow spiritually?" a searching friend recently asked. "I mean, I know that I belong to Jesus, so does it really matter if I mature as a believer?" I know this woman well, and I appreciated her vulnerable questions.

I answered, "Yes, I think it does matter. Scripture is pretty clear about the call to imitate Christ. But beyond that, it depends on what your goals are. My personal goals for my family are peace and laughter. I want to be a person of calmness and joy. I want those attributes to abide in our home. I want my children to know that blessing and be drawn into holiness. The Bible says that peace and joy are attributes of godliness; they come into our lives by the indwelling of the Spirit, and they increase because of maturity."

Galatians 5 says that those characteristics are fruit of the Spirit: "But the fruit of the Spirit is love, joy, peace, patience, kindness, goodness, faithfulness, gentleness and self-control" (vv. 22-23).

But how do we get spiritual fruit? Well, we have to go back to Jesus' words in John 15. We looked at this passage in chapter 2 and heard Jesus calling us to abide in Him. Now look at what happens in the life of a woman who remains with Jesus: She bears fruit.

I am the true vine, and my Father is the gardener. (v. 1)

He cuts off every branch in me that bears no fruit, while every branch that does bear *fruit* he prunes so that it will be even *more fruitful.* (v. 2, emphasis added)

I am the vine; you are the branches. If a man remains in me and I in him, he will bear *much fruit;* apart from me you can do nothing. (v. 5, emphasis added)

This is to my Father's glory, that you bear *much fruit,* showing yourselves to be my disciples. (v. 8, emphasis added)

What is the fruit that Jesus is referring to? Some of the fruit is love, joy, peace, patience, kindness, goodness, faithfulness, gentleness, and self-control—all characteristics of godliness. Do you see the progression in this passage from Galatians? Jesus says that those who remain with Him, those who know Him intimately and grow in maturity, at first bear *fruit* (John 15:2), then *more fruit* (v. 2), and eventually *much fruit* (vv. 5, 8).

That is the reason why we pursue spiritual disciplines. The disciplines of our faith connect us intimately with our Father, the Gardener. They cause us to remain in Him, to abide in His strength and power. These disciplines increase our maturity as well as the spiritual "fruit" in our lives.

Verse 4 says, "No branch can bear fruit by itself." Do you hear that? No mom can become a joyful mom by herself. A mother will not wake up one day and have self-control.

Patience cannot be acquired, nor will gentleness descend on a cloud. There is only one way. The mother who desires the fruit of the spirit must remain in the vine, walking with Jesus. She must intentionally pursue the disciplines that connect her to the Father and fill her soul.

From there, from the fullness of His indwelling and fellowship, the buds of fruit, those attributes that I want with all my heart, will bloom and flourish. Intimacy with God causes the tree of my soul to become ripe with the fruit of godliness. And guess who reaps the benefit of a godly mom? Who gets to enjoy the fruit? All those little seedlings who have sprung up from your tree.

What do kids look like who live with a mom and a dad who run toward God? How do kids turn out when they have been fed the fruit of love, joy, peace, patience, kindness, goodness, faithfulness, gentleness, and self-control? That's what I want to know. I want to know what it looks like to bear spiritual fruit, feed it to my children, and watch it become part of their lives. I want to know what my children will look like because they have had a spiritually mature mother.

So does it really matter if you become a mature woman of God? Absolutely. It matters to your soul, and it matters to those little eyes, what they see ... those little ears, what they hear ... those little feet, where they go.

Our world is hungry for genuinely changed people: moms, dads, and children who have been transformed by the radical power of Jesus. These disciplines of soul care take us into the presence of God so that He can transform us and we can worship Him. Spiritual disciplines are God's means of grace and blessing in our lives. Second Peter 1:3 says, "His divine power has given us everything we need for life and godliness through our knowledge of him who called us by his own glory and goodness."

All the resources are present in Christ. Everything we need to live a godly life is available in Jesus. He is the only answer. He is enough.

Run to Jesus and care for your soul. Do not give up until soul care saturates your life and does its powerful job of healing, restoration, and change. Lean in. Press on. Stay with God until you can say, "It is well, it is well with my soul."

For we do not have a high priest who is

unable to sympathize with our weaknesses,

but we have one who has been tempted

in every way, just as we are—

yet was without sin.

Let us then approach the throne of

grace with confidence, so that we may

receive mercy and find grace to

help us in our time of need.

Hebrews 4:15-16

Chapter Seven

A Woman
of Grace

*W*e were the new church staff family, and I
was six months pregnant, when Cindy
brought a lasagna dinner to our weary tribe on
our first night in Orlando, Florida. Both our families
were waiting for houses to be ready, and Cindy lived two
apartment buildings away. God gave Cindy to me as a neighbor first and then He gave her to me as a friend. We went to
the same church, carpooled together, and walked through
two years of life and mothering. I watched this woman grow
from maturity into greater maturity as we sought the Lord
together.

Five months ago at the time of this writing, God called
Paul to a church in Tennessee. My friend stood with me until
the end. She packed my dishes, painted my walls, cared for
my kids, and brought food to my family while another moving truck loaded up our boxes and pulled away. We cried,

laughed, and said good-bye a hundred times. Finally, one more walk through an empty house, one last hug, and Cindy whispered to me, "Thank you for showing me what it means to live in grace. I will never be the same." Her words still hold me with their encouragement. Perhaps more than anything, I want to be a woman of grace.

Saved, but Graceless

When I first believed in Jesus as my Savior, I thought that I understood grace. I knew that I was a hopeless sinner and that Jesus' love and death for me was grace—an undeserved gift. I did understand grace in part, but only a measure, only a taste. I understood just enough about grace to be saved from my sin, not enough to live and walk in real godliness.

For most of my growing-up years and even into my adult years, I have tried to do the right thing. Doing the right thing may not sound graceless to you, but please read on. The "right thing" can be good, and then it can be oppressive and consuming. The "right thing" can become more about keeping rules and performing for others. Doing the right thing can become a substitute for Christlikeness. For a long time, I mistakenly thought they were the same.

My parents were very gracious parents. I felt completely accepted and loved in our home. But something inside me was driven toward overachievement. Maybe my firstborn tendencies were on hyperdrive, or maybe the junior-high wallflower in me just wanted to prove something to the world. Whatever the motivation, when I came to know Jesus, I turned my energies toward Him and just as intently wanted to "do the right thing" for God.

In my spiritual life, I became a great rule keeper:

Bible reading. Check.

Prayer time. Check.

Scripture memory. Check.

Journal entry. Check.

Church attendance. Check. Check. And double check.

Walking with God? Sure I am! I've got big, fat checks beside all my rules.

What I didn't see were the attitudes that my rules fed. My spirit was secretly haughty and judgmental. My pride increased. My patience with others decreased. I measured my walk with God by performance and knowledge. I am not sure that I really knew anything about grace in those years of spiritual arrogance. I was trying so hard to please God with my spiritual aerobics.

In the summer of 1985, I moved to Dallas, Texas, to begin seminary. During the week before school began, I thought I was going to have a nervous breakdown. Remember, I was the rule keeper and I was asking myself, "How does a godly woman who wants to please God make anything less than an A in Bible or theology? What would it say to God about my love for His Word if I made a C or a D? I have to make A's so that God will know that I love Him." I hope you are laughing at my complete lack of understanding about who God is. I wasn't laughing back then; I was about to freak out.

Needless to say, I dove into seminary headfirst, researching, writing, and reading like a wild woman—acquiring lots of knowledge. I never went to one "Singles Social" because I wanted to be committed to my studies and to ministry. No standing around a punch bowl for me; this was serious business. Oh, the misery of telling you all this ... what a goofball I was!

In those years, we had a running joke about people who

tried too hard. You know the kind: They are the people who cannot just turn in a simple outline on the book of Luke. It has to be illustrated, color coded, and written in calligraphy. We called people like me, and several of my friends who will remain nameless, "excessive repulsive" and laughed about it. "Excessive repulsive" works great in an academic setting, but in the real world, it begins to eat your lunch.

I battled my own personal standards, setting the bar really high, and then suffering alone when I put too much on my plate or flat-out failed. I had sole control over my priorities and circumstances and hung myself time and again. I spent exorbitant amounts of energy trying to do the right thing and be the person I thought everyone expected me to be.

I became a great plate-spinner in my effort to be all things to all people. I was a slave to words like *outstanding, flawless,* and *excellent.* Over time, I began to have the same unrealistic expectations for most everyone else in my life. Privately, I became judgmental, legalistic—actually, quite a good Pharisee (the New Testament version of an excessive repulsive, list maker, rule keeper). I was *doing,* but I was not *becoming.* I lived with only a taste of God's grace, not knowing there was a feast of grace to which I'd been invited.

The Graceless Supermom

Do you know what happens when a cul-de-sac, khaki-clad Pharisee becomes a mother? Well, sometimes she aspires to supermom status. I totally bought in to that fantasy. I don't think I ever said it aloud, but on the inside, I could feel myself rise to the challenge of mothering. I was sure that I could be the best mom to ever pack a diaper bag.

I quietly went to work, observing other Supermoms,

modeling their overachieving techniques, making my own adjustments and improvements so that I could shine even brighter. It was stressful, but I was comfortable in my "excessive repulsiveness." I worked really hard, trying to attain some invisible level of great mothering that always seemed to dangle just outside my reach.

Do you have a mental picture of where I tried to live? Perfect children who always looked and acted like angels ... Do you know how tough it is to get a two-year-old to act like an angel, much less keep her hair bow in? Cute house with laundry that always got done and bathrooms that were never dirty ... It takes a lot of work to keep your house looking as if nobody lives there ... great meals with ease ... entertaining with poise and no preparation ... gardening ... sewing ... a social butterfly. I bought into the whole ball of wax. Needless to say, the harder I worked, the more graceless my life became. The worst part was that now, little eyes watched me do it.

When the Graceless Meet the Grace-Full

I had so much head knowledge about grace, yet little application in my heart. For me, the application began to happen when I spent time with some people who modeled the real grace of God *for* me and *to* me.

A number of years ago, Paul and I lived in Franklin, Tennessee, and every Sunday we sat under the inspired teaching of Scotty Smith at Christ Community Church. Scotty affected my life because he invited me to the feast of God's grace. Week after week, he preached from the Scriptures, he proclaimed the truth of the gospel, and he taught us through word and in life what it means to live redeemed by the power of grace.

Over the years, Scotty led me to the feast of grace where our dear Father abundantly fed my soul. We spent some time around people who weren't so concerned that I did everything right. In fact, the "doing" part of my life didn't impress them at all. They were more concerned with my passion toward God, my brokenness over my sin, and my attitude toward my husband. Through Scotty's teaching and the friends God brought into our lives, I came to understand what it means to be loved "in process." I began to "feel" what grace feels like. I began to "see" what grace looks like. My soul had found its home in the sweet grace of God.

I didn't know I was dry until I got around people who were wet.

—JOANNA WEAVER[1]

At the feast of grace, God set me free. He released me from all my made-up rules. I finally understood that He loved me apart from accomplishment. He accepted me, just me, goofy me, tired-of-trying me—not because of my desire to please Him, but because of His great love and deep affection. Wow. Huge sigh. Deep rest for my soul ... finally, rest for my soul ... safe at home with God.

I was like a captive set free. I was a weary traveler given food and rest. I am still a recovering Pharisee, but I am being changed from encounter to encounter because of the irresistible, transforming grace of God. Once you have tasted the freedom of grace, you will never be satisfied to live without it.

I have learned that you and I can know the Savior and yet

not live in grace. I can recite Scripture, pray as a saint, and yet not live in grace. I can attend church, teach Bible studies, lead people to Christ, outserve the best of them, and yet not live in grace.

God wants us to have more than a taste of grace. He wants us to feast on the riches of His lavish love. Ephesians 1:7-8 says, "In him, we have redemption through his blood, the forgiveness of sins, in accordance with *the riches of God's grace that he lavished on us* with all wisdom and understanding" (emphasis added). The journey of spiritual maturity takes us from the taste into the feast, from the measure into His riches.

The Grace That Comes from Mercy

In Titus, Paul writes a definition of grace: "But when the kindness and love of God our Savior appeared, he saved us, not because of righteous things we had done, but *because of his mercy"* (3:4-5, emphasis added).

Sometimes I will lie awake at night, battling the sinful thoughts in my head, wondering why God would have anything to do with me. Surely there are others more holy or more disciplined. The truth is that there *are* others, and yet God really loves *me.* There are billions of people on this earth, and yet God sees me … hears me … knows me … still loves me. His love comes to me not because I have mastered "doing the right thing," but only because of His mercy. That is the miracle of grace that takes my breath away.

Someone said to me today, "Maybe we just get moments of grace." I could not disagree more. We get a whole lifetime of grace, and then we get grace for all of eternity. That is why it is so indescribable, why it moves us to tears and humility, and why our hearts cannot comprehend its magnitude. Grace is God-sized, and so we cannot wrap our minds around the splendor of this gift. We cannot explain how or why a holy God would continue to pour out His love on an unworthy people. But we do not need to know how or why; we just need to know that it is so.

No matter how much we sacrifice, we cannot make ourselves holy to God. God's standard of holiness is as high as the heavens. Our best efforts will not make us "holy." If we are to be holy, it is only by God's provisions. That's the point! The words holy and pleasing are not conditions of God's acceptance; they are declarations of his mercy.

—Bryan Chapell[2]

Can you hear this? No matter what your feelings of worth before the Father, He loves you now and forever. Grace is the forgiving, redeeming, and pursuing love of God for us. Grace has nothing to do with the things you do or who you are on this earth. The extravagant gift of God's grace comes to us *only* because we belong to God.

That is what makes it so extravagant; we cannot earn it, and yet we so desperately need it.

We cannot make God give us more, because He freely gives us all.

We cannot fall beyond the reach of God's grace, and we cannot grow past our profound need.

We cannot understand the mind of God, so we do not completely comprehend a love that is without boundary or limit. We are awed to know that we can turn away or run away, but God is always, and eternally, still in love with us.

Because of His mercy, we have the privilege of living in this abundance of grace. Some people spend their whole lives striving and searching. Others accumulate accolades and things. But we are most blessed, because the divine grace of God has come to us.

He is here, and by His grace, we can rest.

He is here, and by His grace, we can live.

He is here, and by His grace, we are free.

Free Indeed

In John 8:36, Jesus says, "So if the Son sets you free, you will be free indeed." That is what grace does; it breaks the bondage of sin and loosens the chains of trying so hard and failing so often. Grace sets us free. In this season, we can be free from the burden of Supermom, the expectations of others, a critical spirit, and even the captivity of our own natures.

The Burden of Being Supermom

I don't know who coined the word *Supermom,* but she didn't do the world any favors. Now we have several generations of moms believing that the ability to do everything with extravagance and finesse is the ultimate goal. My heart breaks when I run into moms who are trying so-o-o hard. I see my old graceless, insecure self in their reflection. I want to pull these strangers aside and tell them to take a deep breath ... calm down ... little kids are supposed to get dirty ... dust falls on the furniture of the just and the unjust ... poopy diapers happen. I want the grace of God to free them from the burden of being Supermom.

Just think about the potential for influencing our children if we can live out a legacy of grace. Who is going to reach them with the message of grace if not us? Who else will live the truth that can transform their lives? If grace is easier caught than taught, then our family is where they need to catch it. I figure that I can give my children at least a 20-year head start on their spiritual journey if our home can cultivate grace in their hearts and minds.

Mercy: not getting the penalty that you deserve.
Grace: getting a gift that you don't deserve.

The grace of God will radically transform the whole adventure of motherhood. By grace, we can walk confidently in strength and in peace, resting in being the woman whom God has intended and loving our children well.

Grace makes us less concerned with our children's accomplishments and more concerned with their hearts, helps us forgive them quickly, lets us embrace their differences and applaud their unique creativity, and allows us to laugh with them and laugh at ourselves.

Let me paint a picture for you of a place where the supermom has become a gracious mom:

How to Know Where Grace Lives

You can tell where grace lives because:

- All the neighborhood kids want to hang out at the house where grace lives. There is more dirt to be swept, there are more snacks to be made, and the grass doesn't grow outside the back door or under the swing. But kids show up, hang out, and get loved where grace lives.

- The dust may be a little thicker on top of the TV, and the closets a bit cluttered, but hearts have been tended where grace lives. Family management has become the tool instead of the goal. Schedules matter, but souls matter more.

- There is always enough for one more where grace lives ... one more for dinner ... one more to sleep over ... one more hug ... one more kiss.

- The lights are on late where grace lives. Grace stays up to listen, hug in the dark, and wipe away tears of disappointment and pain.

- You can see people dancing where grace lives, because moms hang up the phone, turn up the music, and dance over the victories of their children. Sometimes the children just watch from behind their cereal and "catch" the grace of a silly mom.

- You can hear things like "Please forgive me, I was wrong ... I'm disappointed, but I love you ... You are my treasure ... You are my blessing ... Let me pray for you."

- The eyes of the children where grace lives shine with joy and anticipation. They have not been wounded by impossible expectations. They have not been distanced by rejection. They have been embraced and accepted and loved.

- The moms at the house where grace lives are just regular, everyday moms, but God lives inside them. By His power, they are becoming holy and righteous and good. They stumble but recover quickly. They make mistakes but say, "I'm sorry." They get blown by the winds of heartache and adversity, but their hearts remain tender toward God.

Read one of my favorite passages about God's tender mercy and grace, Psalm 103:8-14 (emphasis added):

> The LORD is compassionate and gracious, slow to anger, abounding in love. He will not always accuse, nor will he harbor his anger forever; he does not treat us as our sins deserve or repay us according to our iniquities. For as high as the heavens are above the earth, so great is his love for those who fear him; as far as the east is from the west, so far has he removed our transgressions from us. As a father has compassion on his children, so the LORD has compassion on those who fear him; for he knows how we are formed, *he remembers that we are dust.*

I just love that last zinger, "He remembers that we are dust." Do you know what that means for mothers? It means that we can be free from trying to be Supermoms, thinking that we should always be doing more. God knows that we cannot do everything. He formed each of us with only two arms and two legs, one heart and one mind. We cannot be everywhere or do every project.

With our human love and thoughts, we get tired, our patience wears thin, we make mistakes: *We are only dust.* But our God is a compassionate God who loves us in our frailty, and by grace, He casts our sins away and holds us with a heavenly love.

Be encouraged, dear one, there is grace—powerful, *set-you-free-from-bondage kind of grace*—waiting for Supermoms and regular moms and all of us who call Jesus our Lord.

Would you let the grace of God free you from the burden of being Supermom?

Others' Expectations

Many of us spend most of our lives making decisions based on what we think others expect. We live in bondage to their opinions and demands. We live or die by their praise or lack of it. Are we so codependent that being liked supersedes being holy? By grace, we are free to have opinions that run against the grain. We are free to parent according to Scripture instead of according to our society. We are free to search for God's calling in our lives and then pursue His leading. We are free to drive a paid-for minivan with 150,000 miles when everyone else has the latest model.

Grace lets us hear the still, small voice of God, and, no matter what everyone else expects, obey.

When I was in college, we made decisions by committee. If one of us had to make a decision, we would call a meeting in someone's room. Anyone who wandered by the door was fair game for our committee. Whatever the majority decided usually won out because no one wanted to act outside the realm of popular opinion. But by grace, we can grow up and outgrow the need for a committee. We don't have to worry about what everyone else thinks anymore. We can be led by the Holy Spirit, acting on His guidance and resting in the sufficiency of God's love for us. Listen to Paul's words to the Galatians: "Am I now trying to win the approval of men, or of God? Or am I trying to please men? If I were still trying to please men, I would not be a servant of Christ" (Galatians 1:10).

When a mother is free from the bondage of others' opinions, then she can look into the eyes of her child and ask the Lord what is best for that child without being swayed by the newest fads or trends in parenting. She can make tough decisions that may not be popular or cool, because she is operating from the security of God's grace. She can maintain discipline, because she is free from "what everybody else's mother" is doing. She can listen for God, do the absolute best she can, and then rest, because by grace, she has done enough.

Would you let the grace of God free you from others' expectations?

A List of Rules

I have several friends who grew up in alcoholic homes. They tell me that as adult children of alcoholics, they still have this sense that everybody else knows the "list of unwritten rules" for how the world works and they do not. In their homes, logic never worked. They never knew exactly how Mom or Dad was going to respond on a given afternoon. It all depended on the state of their alcoholic parent's sobriety. And now, as adults, these children still find themselves unsure and indecisive in many situations.

I think there are many more of us who are searching for the same unwritten list. We believe there is a list of rules out there, and if we can just find the list and keep all the rules, then life will be happy and good. How about this formerly unwritten list for good mothering:

1. A good mother should prepare homemade, well-balanced meals.
2. A good mother should have the patience of Job with every child and in every situation.
3. A good mother should keep all the clothes clean, ironed, and put away.
4. A good mother should keep the bathrooms and floors free of grime, scuffs, and marks.
5. A good mother should make delicious treats for her children to take to their classrooms and have after school.
6. A good mother should do one craft with her children every day.
7. A good mother should read an intellectually stimulating story to her children every evening.
8. A good mother should never miss a practice, game, or tournament of any sort.
9. A good mother should teach her children good manners, poise, and table etiquette.
10. A good mother should have a great haircut, exercise regularly, and dress fashionably.

Yada, yada, yada.

This list could go on forever. It makes me tired just thinking about it, but I have surprised myself at how quickly I can rattle off these graceless rules for good mothering. I can rattle them off because the list lurks in my heart, ready to pound me if I miss a basketball game or send my child to school in a wrinkled shirt.

The list laughed at me when Grayson came to me this morning and said, "Mommy, you forgot to pack my snack two days in a row." The list of rules sneers at me, "You are not a good mother. You are not a good mother." I must confess, there are moments when I step outside of grace and believe the list. Within every area of my life is the opportunity to search for a list to live by: the list for being a great wife, the list for serving at church, the list for social acceptance. The possibilities are endless, and I hear their accusations trying to pull me away from the feast of grace.

But God draws me back, and grace has the power to free me from all the unwritten lists that want to steal my joy and run my life. Thanks be to God, grace makes life more than a list of rules to keep.

Would you let the grace of God free you from the captivity of lists?

A Critical Spirit

Sometimes in our insecurity, we become critical. Sometimes in our frustration, we become judgmental. Some of us were born, or trained, to see the glass half empty and leaking, but the grace of God is powerful enough to free your heart from a critical spirit.

I firmly believe that there is no place for cutting sarcasm in the Body of Christ, and therefore, there is no place for such sarcasm in my family or in my heart. With petty sarcasm, a few may get a good laugh, but someone always walks away feeling as if she has been tossed a brick.

I have a friend in Florida who lets me tell her story. Janice is tall and stunning, the mother of three beautiful children. She is slim and in great shape. God made Janice very pretty, but she also works hard to take care of herself. Invariably, when I am with Janice in a group of women, someone will usually get in a jab. They will say something like "Janice always looks great. Don't you just hate her?" Everyone else agrees, and then Janice gets to stand there, trying to smile while holding onto the brick they just threw at her. What these women mean as sarcasm, and probably think of as a back-handed compliment, hurts.

We read in Colossians 4:5-6, "Be wise in the way you act toward outsiders; make the most of every opportunity. *Let your conversation be always full of grace,* seasoned with salt, so that you may know how to answer everyone" (emphasis added).

What is petty sarcasm if not the measure of one's insecurity? What is a critical spirit if not the absence of grace? It is mentally and emotionally taxing to search for the negative and wallow in the cynical. How do you feel when you have been with a critical person? I feel drained and exhausted.

Worn out from trying to keep the children in line, I was at my parents' house one afternoon. I had been constantly snapping my finger, clearing my throat, counting to three, putting people in the corner, and giving stern looks. It had been a taxing afternoon, and we were all tired. Later that night, my dad gently said to me, "You know, you don't always have to see *everything* they do wrong." Immediately, the truth of his words deflated my critical heart. I felt myself take a deep breath and exhale while all that negative effort drained out of me. His words of grace were right on target, and they apply across the scope of my life. I do not always have to see everything everybody does wrong. That is grace, and it sets my heart free.

Would you let the grace of God free you from a critical spirit?

Our Natures

Have you ever heard someone blame his or her nature for personal, inconsiderate behavior? It sounds something like this:

- I am a grumpy person and my children know when to leave me alone. It's just my nature.

- I have no patience. I cannot stand to be kept waiting. It's my nature to be punctual, and I expect it from everyone else, no excuses.

- All my coworkers have been informed not to speak to me until I have two cups of coffee. I cannot be civil until I have caffeine.

- I am not a morning person, and I will let my husband have it if he wakes me up before 8:00 A.M. I am a night person by nature.

Now, I certainly understand that we all have our pet peeves and individual preferences. But since when is nature more powerful than grace, especially in the life of a believer? See what these Bible passages have to say about the nature of a Christian:

> Those who live according to the sinful nature have their minds set on what that nature desires; but those who live in accordance with the Spirit have their minds set on what the Spirit desires.... Those controlled by the sinful nature cannot please God. (Romans 8:5, 8)

Therefore, if anyone is in Christ, he is a new creation;
the old has gone, the new has come! (2 Corinthians
5:17)

Christians are changed people. That means by grace we
can be free from our natural inclinations. You still may not be
a morning person, but by the grace of God, you can be nice.
We can use different words, adjust our tone, improve our out-
look. I cringe when I hear a believer say, "I am a grumpy person." Tell me, what is the power of Christ for, if not to change
grumpy people? Grace can overcome grumpy any day of the
week. Radical change is one of God's best things. God's power
is greater than our sinful natures. New creation means that the
old pessimistic, sour, bitter, angry, frustrated, impatient nature
can pass away.

My nightmare was that one of the memories my children
might have of me is the look I have given them while taking
an important phone call. They would follow the phone cord
or my voice coming from the pantry and try to talk to me. It
is frustrating to listen to an adult give me information in one
ear and have two children standing in front of me trying to
tattle. For a quick fix, I would make the most intent, contorted,

Amazing grace: the unlimited favor of an
    almighty God lovingly
    given to the infinitely
    undeserving.

ugly face, communicating very effectively that I could not be spoken to and that they were in big trouble. A few years ago, I realized that my ugly face to my children was completely graceless—a miserable act of my nature. By the grace of Jesus, I am learning to ask the caller to hold, and then I ask my children to wait on the stairs until I am finished. Same frustration, better results, better memories.

Would you let the grace of God free you from your nature?

This chapter was especially difficult to begin. I prayed and cried for days, asking the Lord to come and provide His direction. I sat in front of my blinking computer for over a week and did not keep one word that I had written. I finally realized that the battle was spiritual. Satan does not want mothers to feast at the table of God's grace, because grace will set a mother free and then, yes, she will be free indeed. Free to love her husband well. Free to raise her children in a gracious home. Free to pursue the passions of her heart. Free to stake her whole life on the truth of Christ and run toward His glory.

When you surrender to the sweet call of Jesus, when you fall in love with Him and pursue Him, when you begin to care for your soul, then our God will pour out the riches of His grace upon grace, maturing you as a believer and filling up your life. The disciplines of soul care take us right into the presence of God, and there, in His presence, is amazing grace.

The grace of God is the place where miracles happen, lives change, and relationships get restored. The grace of God sets us free *from* bondage and then frees us *to* enjoy His goodness and blessing.

In the next chapter we will explore the blessings that wait for the woman who cannot be satisfied with a measure. Her soul has been awakened, and she will not be content until she moves from the taste of grace on to the feast.

Grace runs downhill to the humble.

—JACK MILLER[3]

But when the kindness and love of

God our Savior appeared, he saved us, not

because of righteous things we had done, but

because of his mercy

… so that, having been justified by his grace,

we might become heirs having

the hope of eternal life.

Titus 3:4-5, 7

And God is able to make all grace

abound to you, so that in all things

at all times, having all that you need,

you will abound in every good work.

2 Corinthians 9:8

Chapter Eight

Grace upon Grace

*D*o you remember the years before your children? Did you ever look at a mother and wonder how she did it? Did you ever ask yourself, "Where does the 'want to' come from?" Did you doubt that you could? I did.

I could not understand how a woman could step from the world of self into the world of mothering with such complete devotion. After four children, I still do not understand, except to say that being possessed by a mother's love is *supernatural.* It is the unconditional love of God poured through me into my children.

For women who know Jesus Christ as their Lord, motherhood is an ongoing, penetrating lesson in grace. We begin with only a measure of grace, but through the years and experiences that grow us up, God leads us into His riches. God comes into our lives through our babies and begins the powerful work of change.

He is teaching me, leading me, guiding me, and calling me. Through my children, He has taken me by the hand and led me to a selfless place where I could have never gone by myself. On the path of spiritual maturity He gives grace, then more grace, and finally abundant grace so that I can give to my children from the wealth of His goodness.

My sister-in-law, Kim, e-mailed me "A Tribute to Moms." I think it captures the truth of God's love and grace being poured out through ordinary women. It speaks to all of us who are being transformed in our everyday lives by the supernatural gift of mother love and abundant grace. Here is a portion:

A TRIBUTE TO MOMS

This is for all the mothers who froze their bottoms off on metal bleachers at soccer games Friday night instead of watching from cars, so that when their kids asked, "Did you see my goal?" they could say, "Of course, I wouldn't have missed it for the world," and mean it.

This is for all the mothers who have sat up all night with sick toddlers in their arms, wiping up chunks of wieners and cherry soda that suddenly reappeared saying, "It's okay honey, Mommy's here."

This is for all the mothers of Kosovo who fled in the night and can't find their children.

This is for the mothers who gave birth to babies they will never see ... and the mothers who took those babies and made homes for them.

This is for the mothers of victims of school shooting ... and the mothers of the murderers ... for the mothers of the survivors, and the mothers who sat in front of their TVs in horror, hugging their child who just came home from school safely.

This is for all the mothers who run carpools and make cookies and sew Halloween costumes ... and all the mothers who don't.

This is for reading "Goodnight, Moon" twice a night for a year ... and then reading it again, "just one more time."

This is for all the mothers who mess up, who yell at their kids in the grocery store and stomp their feet like a tired two-year-old who wants ice cream before dinner.

This is for all the mothers who taught their daughters to tie their shoelaces before they started school ... and for all the mothers who opted for velcro instead.

This is for all the mothers who show up at work with spit-up in their hair, milk stains on their blouses, and diapers in their purse.

This is for all the mothers who teach their sons to cook and their daughters to sink a jump shot.

—AUTHOR UNKNOWN

I have added my own words to this tribute:

Dear working mom, stay-at-home mom, single mom, married mom, mothers without, and mothers with everything, God sees you. He knows you. He loves you. You are His hands of love, His arms of compassion, and His gift of grace to the next generation.

I read these words in my e-mail late one night and cried unto sobs. I am still moved when I recount the depth of love and the potential for heartache in these simple lines about the everyday tasks of mothering.

What makes my lip quiver and the lump jump into my throat when I think about the power of a mother's love? I cry because being a mother is such a privilege. I cry because I forget that it is a privilege. I cry because I love my children so. I cry because I want to love them more. I cry because I sense in my soul that this love transcends all my understanding. I cry because I am humbled to be the vessel entrusted with their care.

When I think about the grace that mothering requires, I am amazed that I have any at all, and yet, by faith in Christ Jesus, you and I are being given a supernatural grace, a grace that causes us to love and protect, a grace that brings us to tears when we consider its magnitude.

The New Way Called Grace

If we are the vessels of grace to our children, and we are, and if mothering requires more grace than we possess, and it does, then as followers of Christ, we must remain intimately connected to the Giver of grace. Only there will our need for more grace be supplied. We read in John 1:14:

The Word became flesh and made his dwelling among us. We have seen his glory, the glory of the One and Only, who came from the Father, full of grace and truth.

And then in verse 16 (NASB):

For of His fullness we have all received, and grace upon grace.

When Jesus came into this dark world, He came in the glory of grace and truth, a glory that represented the very presence of God. He came into a world full of rules and regulations and ministered in a new way. He alone introduced a revolutionary way of life called grace. The religious people of His day had been in bondage to rules and lists, entrenched in a lifestyle of religious "excessive repulsive" because of guilt and duty. When Jesus came, His grace heaped upon grace freed the religious captives: They were set free from the rules and answered the call to follow their Lord simply out of love and devotion.

And God raised us up with Christ and seated us with him in the heavenly realms in Christ Jesus, in order that in the coming ages he might show the incomparable riches of his grace, expressed in his kindness to us in Christ Jesus.

—EPHESIANS 2:6-7

He did not focus on the letter of the law or the accomplishments of the followers. Jesus taught a new way, focusing on the heart. He replaced requirements with a relationship. He exchanged the law for faith. And today, the power of His grace has not diminished. His provision of grace has the authority to set us free *from* the shackles of bondage, but grace also frees us *to* live in the bounty of God's abundance: God's grace upon grace.

In this chapter we are going to look at the riches of God's grace that have come through His Son, Jesus, a gift that is simply ... amazing.

The Riches of Grace

Because of Jesus' example and teaching, you and I are free to enjoy life to its very fullest. We can fulfill our roles as mothers, forgive others, set aside worry about the future, and much more. Let's dive into some of the freedoms grace provides for mothers.

Love, Laugh, and Live

Most of us have forgotten how to love, laugh, and live. The world has come up to meet us, and the phrase "Life is tough" begins to speak volumes. There are mortgages, school shootings, world hunger, and unreached people groups. There is sickness, divorce, the homeless, and corporate downsizing. Life can get all too solemn, gloomy, and grim. In between managing our mutual funds, working at the women's shelter, and coordinating the silent auction at school, we can begin to take ourselves too seriously. We hear ourselves say things like "When the baby is out of diapers ... when all the children are in school ... when we have a bigger house ... when we have more money." Then, before we know it, a decade has flown by and we still have not laughed very much and have enjoyed very little. It becomes easy to focus on tomorrow or next year, altogether missing today.

I say to you, O serious mother, by the grace of God, today is the day to dance and to sing! These are the days to hug long and love loud. Grab somebody and hold onto them past the polite hug. Rescue your teenager from her geometry homework, turn on the kids' music, and learn to dance again. Serve dinner for the whole family in the tree fort. Today is the day that God has given to you, and grace sets you free to savor it and pass on the joy.

Do you know what it means to "love loud"? My friend Barbara taught me this great lesson many years ago. I was new in town, and Barbara was the fun and creative wife of a respected executive. It seemed that everyone knew Barbara and her husband. She and I met one day and really seemed to connect, but I assumed that because of her huge circle of friends, our connection would be forgotten.

A few weeks later I was at a large meeting where about four hundred women were mingling in the sanctuary of a local church. I spotted Barbara across the room with women all around her and many waiting to talk to her. She was obviously loved and admired. I chose not to bother her and let myself fade into the sea of the unknown, smiling cordially at the other women, who all seemed to have friends. Silently I sulked in my aloneness.

Then over the dull roar of chattering, I heard, "An-ge-la, heeeeeey, Angela come over here. I am so glad to see you. Let me introduce you." It was Barbara, and she was waving and yelling to me … to me. Everyone had turned to see who Barbara was calling. I think I floated over to her with a huge, goofy grin on my face. Barbara loved me loud, and it made me feel like a princess.

I am learning to love loud. Do you want to see somebody's face light up? Remember people's names. Call your friend's name from a long way off, wave to her, and hug her long when you get to her. Don't avoid your neighbor because your hair looks gross. Go to her and speak to her. Your love and sincerity will overcome even the worst hair day. Lead with your heart, and people won't notice your hair.

To love loud might mean that you rejoice with your friends when they rejoice (Romans 12:15). We are very good at weeping with those who weep, but the Body of Christ has a lot to learn about rejoicing. Whenever someone calls me to tell me she is pregnant or some other wonderful news, I want her to know that I rejoice with her. I whoop and holler with that person. I sing and praise God with her. Have you ever had great news to tell, only to be rained on by some friend's halfhearted response? There is nothing like an indifferent attitude to drown your joy. We do the happy dance in our house over wonderful news and success. Find a way to celebrate the goodness of God, and pass it on.

Push past the envelope of your comfort zone and stomp on your insecurity. Stop waiting for someone to notice you and be the one who initiates. Too many of us are waiting to be loved, when God has called us to be the lovers, to give the joy that we have been given. You have been freed by the grace of God to help others enjoy their lives.

In our family we honk the horn to say, "I love you." One Sunday night after church, I had all the kids in the minivan, and we were driving by the front of the church, where people were standing to talk. I spotted Paul, who had stayed for a meeting, and so I rolled down the window to wave and yell. Then I honked the horn. I decided to lay on the horn for a few miles. The kids were laughing and yelling but finally said, "Mom, I don't think he can hear us anymore."

Later that week, I saw a couple of college students who had been talking to Paul. One of them said, "Paul says all that horn honking means 'I love you.'"

I said, "Yes, it does."

"Oh," he said. "We thought your horn was stuck." We both laughed, but what mattered is that Paul heard me love him loud.

This weekend I am praying for a woman who has not told her 13-year-old daughter "I love you" in four or five years. I spent an hour with her recently, and we talked about how devastating it could be for this daughter if the mother continues to withhold her "out-loud love." At everyone's core is an insecure person who can be made secure by the loud love of family and friends. At the center of this mom is a woman with an empty soul, holding out her cup to all the wrong places. She is at a choosing place now. She can choose to embrace the fullness of Christ and the freedom to say "I love you" again, or she can stay trapped in the pain and shackles of her graceless life.

I know that life is difficult and painful. I know that most of us are limited by finances and energy. But I also know that your attitude toward life can be transformed. We are faced with many sad and serious days, but every moment does not have to be so. By the grace of God, you and I are made free to live and love, to enjoy and to celebrate. We can laugh again. We can play. We can hug long and love loud. We can live with greater fervor.

Would you let the grace of God set you free to live and laugh and love again?

Be the Mommy

I was standing in my kitchen one afternoon a few years ago, completely frustrated by constant interruptions, bickering, and the ongoing pressures of my children. That day in the kitchen was not a new day. I was feeling the stress and anxiety I had experienced almost since I first leaped into motherhood. I had been pestered with thoughts like *Maybe I shouldn't have become a mother. I don't do a very great job* and *I must not be cut out for this or I wouldn't be so frustrated.* On the inside, I could not get to a patient or peaceful place. It seemed as though my care for the children was always hurried. At least, I felt hurried on the inside, trying to take care of them so that I could get back to the thing I wanted to do.

That afternoon was like most every other afternoon. I had been saying to the children, "Hang on ... just a minute ...

Mommy's trying to fix dinner ... I'll do that in a little while."
But for some reason that day, the most clear thought came into
my head: "Angela, would you stop fighting being the mother?"

The surprise of that thought shocked me with its pointed
truth. In my spirit, I had been fighting being the mother. At
some level, I felt my life was inconvenienced and interrupted
by mothering. In those moments, I realized that my children
were not the source of my frustration—it was my attitude
toward my children.

I turned off the stove and went to them. I bent down and
tied their shoes. I wiped their faces and looked into their eyes.
They brought me books, and we sat on the floor and read. I
literally felt the tension drain from my body and the peace of
God descend. Nothing else mattered except hearing their
words and watching their "Mommy, look at me" theatrics. It
felt good to stop fighting inside and let my spirit be still.

The lesson that began that day is a lesson of grace. Being a
mommy is both a gift and a burden. The responsibilities are
never-ending and sometimes feel all-consuming. Yet the day
will be won or lost, not based on my accomplishment, but
based on my attitude. The grace of God can set my attitude
free to be the mommy. By His grace, my frustrations can be
replaced with peace. By His grace, I can speak calmly and listen
patiently. By His grace, I can forsake my to-do list and play
with my children. By His grace, I can celebrate this season
called *Mommy.*

Would you let the grace of God set you free to be the mommy?

Forgive

One sure way to stay the way you are, to continue in the mire
and muck of a weak spiritual life, is to live without the grace
of forgiveness. Listen to the Scriptures:

All the prophets testify about him that everyone who believes in him receives forgiveness of sins through his name. (Acts 10:43)

If we confess our sins, he is faithful and just and will forgive us our sins and purify us from all unrighteousness. (1 John 1:9)

For if you forgive men when they sin against you, your heavenly Father will also forgive you. But if you do not forgive men their sins, your Father will not forgive your sins. (Matthew 6:14-15)

Bear with each other and forgive whatever grievances you may have against one another. Forgive as the Lord forgave you. (Colossians 3:13)

Because of grace, you and I are free to receive God's forgiveness. We want to work for it, but we cannot. We want to suffer long enough to be worthy, but we cannot. We are ashamed of our sin, but God sees it no more. By grace, we can receive the gift of His forgiveness, be cleansed of our sin, and begin the next moment freed by His glory.

In the same way, the Lord has commanded us to forgive those who have caused us heartache and pain. The same principle applies. They cannot work for it long enough to earn it. They cannot suffer deeply enough to be worthy of our forgiveness. To forgive another person is an act of obedience to God, a step of spiritual maturity, a measure of grace.

There is power in forgiveness. Anger locks you in, but the lock is on the inside. The grace of God gives you the key that opens the lock. When you realize that anger is destroying your life, you *can* decide to get healthy. You can take the key of grace and let yourself out through forgiveness.

There is a line I remember about forgiveness, and it always gives me perspective. It says, "You will never be asked to forgive anyone more than God has already forgiven you."

Would you let the grace of God free you to forgive yourself and forgive others?

Entrust and Stop Worrying

To entrust means to transfer the responsibility of something valuable to a place of safekeeping. Second Timothy 1:12 says, "I ... am convinced that he is able to guard what I have entrusted to him."

What do you regard as valuable? Your marriage? Your children? Your home and belongings? Your career? Your friends? Your future? God knows that all these things are valuable to you, and they are valuable to Him as well. But how do you hold onto your valuables? Do you hold on with tightly clenched fists, or do you hold them with open hands?

When we hold with our hands open, then we can entrust our treasure to the Lord. This scripture says that *He is able to guard* every person and thing that you cherish. With our hands open, He is able to replace good with better without the painful process of prying our fists apart. He is free to work His will in our lives because we trust that He is able.

By the grace of God, you can entrust your stuff to the Lord and believe that He is better suited to care for your treasure. You do not have to worry or fret. Believe Psalm 55:22: "Cast your cares on the LORD and *he will sustain you*" (emphasis added).

Under the weight of our tightly held treasures, we suffer as if we are all alone, bearing the load of worry and pain. But

Paul says in Galatians 2:20, "I have been crucified with Christ and I no longer live, but Christ lives in me." Do you hear Paul's words? Christ lives in you. You are not by yourself anymore. It may *feel* lonely out here in Mommy land, but we are not alone. We have not been put in a rowboat all by ourselves and told to find our way to shore. Christ is with us and in us. He is able to carry every burden and faithful to sustain us in every trial. He is worthy of our trust.

We live far below our possibilities because we do not hand over our burdens and our treasures. The secret of the gospel is that it is not just me anymore; it is *Christ in me*. We do not have to live as if we are in the boat alone. By the sweet grace of God, we can entrust with complete confidence. We can lay our worries and our cares at the cross of Christ; we can have victory over fears and anxiety.

Would you let the grace of God set you free to entrust and stop worrying?

Smile at the Future

One of my favorite lines in the famous Proverbs 31 passage says that this woman of many talents "can smile at the future" (v. 25). Do you know why she can smile at the future in all its

Hope, in its properly Christian sense, means a sure and confident expectation that what has been promised to us will finally blossom in all its wonderful glory.

—ALISTER MCGRATH[1]

uncertainty? She can smile because she knows that the One who holds the future holds her.

You may be like me and come from a long line of worriers. You may even bill yourself as a professional worrier, hand wringer, and nail biter. My friend, I have a great place for all that nervous energy: the sweet and safe haven of God. May you know with all certainty:

that our Father is your protector,

that our Father is your keeper,

that our Father is your refuge.

Lift up those downcast eyes. Release those worried lines from your face. Turn that pensive frown into the glorious smile of a woman of grace—a woman who knows the God of all eternity and believes that He loves her.

Would you let the grace of God set you free to smile at the future?

More Than Enough

Perhaps the most often quoted Bible verse about grace is 2 Corinthians 12:9, where Jesus says to Paul and to us, "My grace is sufficient for you, for my power is made perfect in weakness." Then Paul goes on to say:

> Therefore I will boast all the more gladly about my weaknesses, so that Christ's power may rest on me. That is why, for Christ's sake, I delight in weaknesses, in insults, in hardships, in persecutions, in difficulties. For when I am weak, then I am strong. (2 Corinthians 12:9-10)

In motherhood, I have come to know the weakest parts of myself. I see where other moms are more and I am less. I feel the weight of wanting to be all and struggling to be in part. There are more hardships and difficulties than I could have ever anticipated. To love one man well, raise children, care for a home, and pursue my passions is to be confronted with the truth of my weakness. I am not enough. I cannot possibly do it all.

But then Jesus speaks and says, "There—right there in the weakness of motherhood—there is where my power is perfected. My grace in you will be more than enough." And I can rest. I can breathe a deep sigh of relief and rest. The power of Christ covers my weak places and supernaturally makes me strong.

Paul also testifies to the power of Christ in 2 Corinthians 4:7-10:

> But we have this treasure in jars of clay to show that this all-surpassing power is from God and not from us. We are hard pressed on every side, but not crushed; perplexed, but not in despair; persecuted, but not abandoned; struck down, but not destroyed. We always carry around in our body the death of Jesus, so that the life of Jesus may also be revealed in our body.

Paul wants us to know that weak vessels—jars of clay, regular moms like us—give great testimony to the all-surpassing power of God. We testify by our lives that any strength we have comes from God and not from us.

We are *hard pressed on every side* by the sheer demands of our families and lives, but by the grace of God, we will not be crushed.

Daily we may find ourselves *perplexed*, searching for answers to the world's questions, but by grace, we will not despair.

We may be *persecuted* by our finances, our work, and even our families, but by the grace of God, we have not been abandoned.

We may get up every morning, only to feel *struck down* by the world and the pain around us, but by the grace of God, we will not be destroyed.

We carry the power of Jesus in our bodies, and He promises that His grace will be enough.

But how do you and I get to grace? The only way I know to get to the grace of God is to go back to soul care. If the cup of your soul is empty, you cannot walk in the grace of God. Sometimes I begin by just lying on my face and asking the Lord to come and minister to me. In my weakness, I may cry or even feel angry, but I lie there and pray until He comes and covers me with His grace.

He will come. He always does. And in His presence, you will move from a measure of grace into His riches … from a taste into the feast.

Grace will take a hard woman and make her soft. Grace can make an angry woman glad. Grace forgives the unforgiven. Grace buries grudges. Grace loves the unlovely. Grace sees potential when the world sees none. Grace looks past the blemishes again and again and again.

Grace always hopes,
  always dreams,
    always believes,
      always tries.

Grace doesn't give up on anybody for any reason.

When a mother grabs hold of the grace of God, then by

that power, she is set free. She is free to forgive herself and her family. She is free to see what really matters in life and then run after it. She is free to laugh with her children and to embrace the quirks of her husband. She is free to endure hardship and suffering, to look past the flaws and rejoice over success, to search for her passions, and to be content in God's provision.

Don't you want to be free? Then by grace, our Jesus says, you shall be free indeed.

Maybe you have just gotten your feet wet in the water of grace. Turn around and see that there is an ocean around you.

Wade in a little deeper.

Ride the waves.

Dive in.

We cannot be satisfied to only get our feet wet when God is calling us to bathe in the ocean of His love called grace.

He has showed you, O man, what is good.

And what does the LORD require of you?

To act justly and to love mercy

and to walk humbly with your God.

MICAH 6:8

Chapter Nine

Passionate Contentment

*P*aul and I went to see *The Phantom of the Opera* several years ago when it came to Nashville. The staging was spectacular, the music was masterful, and the fantastic production kept us riveted to our seats the entire evening. After this wonderful performance, the curtains were drawn back and each actor was introduced. From the shadows, each one ran at full speed to the front of the stage to take his or her bow. As the greater roles were introduced, the applause became thunderous. We whistled and hollered and clapped until our hands hurt … and I cried.

One summer, Paul was interviewing for a new job in Florida, and we were staying at a beautiful hotel in Orlando. It was my birthday, so he woke me early to go down for breakfast. At exactly 7:32 A.M., we were ordering omelettes when the space shuttle re-entered our airspace en route to landing at

Cape Canaveral. I don't know if you have ever heard the space shuttle re-enter our atmosphere, but it will rock your world. Two enormous sonic booms sound out its safe return from the amazing trip just taken into space. The astronauts were home safely … and I cried.

Our daughter Taylor went to her first summer camp recently. At the end of the week, all the parents were invited to come and watch the closing festivities. A few hundred girls stood on their chairs and chanted every camp chant ever written. They stood arm-to-arm and praised God in their loudest voices. They held lit candles as high as their arms would stretch and proclaimed their renewed commitment to love and serve our Jesus. Our nine-year-old had just experienced the most passionate week of her whole life. We stood in the back and watched her shine … and I cried.

Nothing moves me more than the privilege of witnessing great passion. When outstanding actors run onto the stage for their deserved applause, I am moved by their commitment and gifts. I applaud the determination that took them from an audition into long rehearsals and onto a grinding tour so that they could finally do what they were made to do.

I am moved by the devotion and rigorous training that is required of men or women before they can be proclaimed astronauts. The courage that rockets them beyond gravity in a matter of minutes, and then brings them home safely, makes my heart well up with pride and gratitude for their gifts.

And then, when a group of kiddos get passionate about anything, especially Jesus, and one of those kiddos is mine, well, I can hardly contain myself. I am inspired by their energy and the joy of watching them taste passion.

I love being around when people are exercising their gifts, doing those things for which they were created. Watching them do something great wakes me up. To walk through a beautifully kept garden, to run my fingers across the fine cabinetry of a master craftsman, to close my eyes and listen to an anointed voice sing straight from heaven, to hear a man preach the truth of Scripture from the well of study and the power of the Holy Spirit, to sit in the stands and watch those great athletes called TarHeels move with finesse and precision, to watch a skillful teacher unravel a truth until it is grasped by the kindergartner's mind—I am drawn to the passion of each. I am inspired to be passionate. Energy and skill, practice and perseverance, aspiring, training, becoming—these traits perk up my spirit and call me toward an intentional life.

But just about the time I get inspired, thinking that God has put something passionate inside of me, the world marches in and screams, "Wait a cotton-pickin' minute! What is all this aspiring, gifted, intentional stuff? You are a mother. You have four small children, for goodness' sake. You do not have time to be passionate about anything that does not involve a husband, a home, and kids. If you want to be passionate about homeschooling, fine. If you want to be passionate about soccer, fine. If you want to be passionate about cooking, okay. But do not think about searching your soul to find anything else. You do not have the time, energy, or resources to pursue the passions of your heart. Don't you need to iron or something? Now get these crazy ideas out of your head."

Many days, I am tired, and it is easier to believe the world.

Holding onto the Thread

When I go to bed at night, I often lie there for a moment and unwind the day in my head. I try to pray back through the day and into the next one. Frequently I am asleep before "amen," but every once in a while, I will lie there long enough to remember my passions. I will think about that thing inside me that gives me energy, that part of me that has been stamped with individual purpose. Some people refer to these passions as *callings*. And usually, it feels as if I am only holding onto a tiny thread. But I clutch it tightly and hold it up to God, praying to Him, "Lord, here is the passion that You have given to me. It is only a thread in my hands right now, but I have found it and I will hold onto it. I will not let it go."

The primary call on my life is to bring glory to my heavenly Father. I have also been called to be Paul's wife and my children's mother. These are my prevailing callings, but they are not the callings to which I refer. There are passions and gifts inside each one of us that extend beyond the circles of being a wife and mother. I know some people will disagree with me, but I believe that a woman can be a mother and a wife and still pursue the other passions that God has put inside her heart.

The difficulty is that mothering, and even marriage, is about sacrifice and otherness. We have stopped dreaming for ourselves and begun dreaming for these new lives. We have buried our passion because it got in the way, or we stopped looking for it because we had no time. We have deferred our calling until we "get all the kids in college," or we have transferred it into their lives, hoping to live it vicariously through them.

Somewhere inside of you there is at least a thread of passion, a divine thread put there by God. It defines who you are and is a part of the reason you were created. Do you sense the yearning for passion in your spirit? Do you long to find the thread that has been woven through your life? This chapter is about finding that thread and holding onto it in this season.

Eventually, a thread of passion, in the hands of our almighty God, will become the beautiful tapestry of a fruitful life.

Two Camps

There are two women standing in my kitchen having a discussion about passion. One says, "I have given up everything for my children. I decided that it was more important to play with them and for them to know me than for me to hold onto my passions. I never wanted them to be able to say that I was too busy for them. Maybe I have held onto a thread, but I consciously decided to be more passionate about them than anything else in my life."

The second mom says, "There are so many things that I feel passionate about. My children are my greatest calling, but I do not want to sacrifice every ounce of me on the altar of motherhood. I want the thread of my passion and more. Balancing is my struggle."

Two camps, two committed mothers, two ideas about motherhood and passion, two thoughtful women who have reached different conclusions. There is a good possibility that the first mom does not need this chapter. She has gladly chosen to lay down everything for her children. They are her sole passion. For her, she has chosen correctly. I fall into the second camp with the next mom. I figure that I spend about 95 percent of my life providing for my family, caring, loving, and pouring myself into them. For me, the question is not how to get more time away from my family. I want them to have the whole 95 percent. The question I ask myself is, "How can I bring glory to God with the remaining 5 percent? Will I squander that time and energy, or will I use that small portion to pursue my passions?"

I am choosing my passions. I do not get to choose them often, nor do I get around to that 5 percent of my life every day. But I believe that God wired me with some gifts that He intended I use for His glory. Passions do not have to separate us from our roles as wives and mothers. We do not have to forsake one in order to pursue the other. I cannot imagine turning away from my family in order to "do my own thing." In my heart, I know that God is calling me to pursue those passions even in my season of motherhood.

Before we can get to passions, we must take a look at the companion of your passion: your purpose.

God's Purpose in You

Some people go through their whole lives and never really come to realize God's purpose for them. Does that scare you? It sure does me. I do not want to get to heaven and have God say, "Good job, Angela, but you missed so much. I had a lot more in mind for you. You had incredible potential, but you buried the talent I gave you. What did you think those passions were for? I put them there. I gave you gifts that you never unwrapped." One of my greatest fears on this earth is that I would finish my life and miss the heart of God's intent and purpose for me, that I would not hear His voice.

How awful to reach the end of life's road and find we haven't brought our hearts along with us.

—John Eldredge[1]

Keep in mind that it is easier to hear the voice of God when you meet with Him. From a spiritual distance, we become hard of hearing. We cannot discern or decide how the Lord is leading. We cannot distinguish His voice from everyone else's. We cannot identify the strengths and gifts He has built into our personalities. We cannot find our passions. I must care for my soul and walk with my Savior if I want to hear His voice and know His will.

If we were to build a grid that helped to filter God's purpose for our lives, we would probably use four guidelines:

The first piece of the grid is laid because you belong to God. Because of your relationship with Jesus, you can know that your purpose will have to do with holiness and heavenly thinking. Consider these passages:

And we know that in all things God works for the good of those who love him, who have been *called according to his purpose.* (Romans 8:28)

[Our Lord] has saved us and *called us to a holy life*— not because of anything we have done but because of his own purpose and grace. This grace was given to us in Christ Jesus before the beginning of time. (2 Timothy 1:9)

Therefore, holy brothers, who share in the *heavenly calling,* fix your thoughts on Jesus, the apostle and high priest whom we confess. (Hebrews 3:1)

Heaven and holiness and God have everything to do with your purpose here. If you had considered that the plan for your life has nothing to do with God, you have been terribly misled. You are a child of God, and that will have everything to do with your purpose. I am a child of my parents. I look like them and act like them. I bear the strengths and limitations they have given to me. I will never be anyone but the firstborn of Joe and Novie Thomas. In just the same way, I will always be the child of my Savior, bearing the strengths and passions He has given to me.

God's purpose for you has to do with knowing that He is your full cup. He is all you need. The first part of our grid is woven with the call to holiness and heavenly thinking.

The second part of the grid is your distinct design. You are distinctly feminine and you are a mother. Genesis 1:27 reads, "So God created man in his own image, in the image of God he created him; male and female he created them."

We were made in the image of God, and we were made different from men. One of the highest items on the feminist agenda seems to be to nullify role distinctions, but God created us differently on purpose. He also created us equal. We do not have to listen to a culture that says, "You have to be the same as a man to have value." We can celebrate our distinct design as feminine. We can give honor to the role of motherhood in our lives. Our purpose will filter through the grid of our femininity and mothering.

The third piece in this grid is your personality. I am doing some fascinating reading by author Cynthia Tobias about children's learning styles. Isn't it interesting to look at the differences in our own children and embrace them? In the same way, our Lord embraces your personality and uses it for His holy purpose. Jeremiah 1:5 says, "Before I formed you in the womb I knew you, before you were born I set you apart; I appointed you as a prophet to the nations."

Thankfully, God knew us before we were born and fashioned our purpose with our personalities in mind. He knows every extrovert and every introvert, and the Type A's from the Type B's. He has always known about temperaments and takes great delight in both the melancholy and the sanguine. He will not call you to a purpose that your personality cannot embrace.

The final piece of our grid is the powerful emotion of your passions. Passion has been defined as "the object of your boundless enthusiasm" and "the voice of gladness inside your soul." Your passion probably will not be a new revelation. The thread of your passion has already been woven through most of your life experiences. Your passion will be a part of the compass that guides you to your purpose.

We can use this grid to filter the decisions and choices that bombard our days. We can say no to great opportunities because they do not filter through the grid of our purpose. We can say yes with greater enthusiasm and confidence to those choices that sift through. Whatever filters through and falls out the bottom is probably a good fit with who you are and God's design for your life.

The Thrill of Discovery

"I could do anything, if I just knew what it was," I once heard a woman proclaim. Most of us have probably felt like that woman at one time or another. We long to know what we were made for, if we could only figure it out. *Others seem to know with such assurance. Why can't I know? Why is it so challenging to know my own strengths and gifts? Why can't I know my passions?*

When people talk about passions, they generally ask questions such as "What makes you want to get up early and stay up late? What makes your heart race and your spirit soar? What makes you glad?" When I am having a difficult "mommy day," I could easily respond to these questions like this: "Nothing makes me want to get up early or stay up late. I am exhausted. Sleep is precious. My spirit soars when I get the laundry put away. An empty dishwasher makes me glad. Don't ask me these questions. They are too hard and I am too tired to think. Please do not add one more thing to my life."

When safety and prosperity become our passions, we can be sure we've abandoned the pursuit of our God-given destiny in favor of a sub-standard life. If we were honest, we'd have to admit that this attitude is one of pure and simple fear. We don't take risks, we don't dream about doing great things because we're afraid that if we don't protect ourselves and our stuff, we'll lose what's ours—or what we think is ours. Ironically, we are never more vulnerable than when we are playing it safe.

—BILL AND KATHY PEEL[2]

These are thoughtful questions, and my impulsive comeback could protect me from considering their weight, but that is not my heart's desire. Deep down inside, I do want to know that part of me. I want to know what I am made for. I want to operate in my strengths and my passions.

Several years ago, an innocent comment connected with my soul, and today it still fuels my desire for a passionate life. I had been living in Texas for a few months and called back home to talk to a dear friend. I was single, and she had been married for a few years. The conversation unexpectedly waned, so I stepped up with enthusiasm and asked, "What is the most exciting thing that has happened to you in the past few months?"

My friend stumbled verbally and finally came up with, "Well, um, well, we got a new screen door last week."

I waited for more, but nothing else came. My heart sank to my toes. That was it? That was the most exciting thing she could come up with? I do not remember anything else she said, but after I got off the phone, I vowed to God that as long as I am able, I will live every good day and every hard day with passion and heart. Now, 15 years later, I still ask God to protect me from the "screen door."

Back then I knew that if God was going to save me from the "screen door," I had to find out what my passions were. I began to read and listen to others who were talking about passions. Many times the theme of childhood came up. "What did you enjoy doing as a child?" That question always puzzled me. I lived in a house behind that of my younger cousin Cindy, and for as much of my childhood as I can remember, I willingly did whatever Cindy told me to do. I wanted to go wherever she wanted to go, and I wanted to play whatever game she wanted to play. Mustard sandwiches were a defining moment for me. I decided that I did not like them just because Cindy did. Slowly and very timidly, I began to choose according to my heart, and one of those choices was cheerleading.

I loved cheerleading. I loved to practice and learn new cheers. I loved teaching new routines and working on them until we dropped. I cheered my heart out no matter what. Even when my team was losing badly, I gave it everything until the last whistle. A few years later, I worked with a group called ACT I and taught them choreography. Again, that joy of teaching was resurrected. I absolutely loved planning and breaking each dance apart step by step until even the least skilled could do it. The thread of my passion had been woven.

As I looked back at my great gladness in both of those areas, the truth of my passion began to emerge. My passion is teaching the Scriptures to women and using that relationship to guide them toward maturity. I get so excited about women who are growing up in Christ. I love watching the spiritual lightbulbs come on and seeing lives change because of Jesus. Sometimes I still feel like a cheerleader: "Come on, sister, you can do it! Put a little power to it!"

Since I have locked on, the Lord has often reaffirmed the passion He gave me for teaching. At 24, I made one of the most difficult decisions of my life. I left a great job in my father's company to go to seminary. For at least a year I wrestled with the desire to be with my father in corporate America and the passion for God's Word that seemed to burn inside me.

One day I sat teary-eyed in the office of Kathleen Simmons, my father's "right hand" and secretary. She was a godly woman, and that day I was pouring out my confusion. I said, "Aunt Kat, if I told you that I was going to give up all this, all the security and potential of this job, and go to seminary, would you think I'm crazy?"

Kathleen replied, "Angela, if at your young age you know what you want to live for, you have more than most of us have at 50. Go do what God is calling you to do and don't look back." A few months later, I went on to seminary.

I have met many passionate people. They come in all ages, from all backgrounds, with all sorts of personal capacities. No two look alike. But you know them when you see them. They are not hurried; they are not shrill; they are not out to impress.

You know them because when you come into their presence, they make you think of Christ. Somehow you feel that you have just understood a little more of what it was like to be in the presence of Jesus.

The energy that pushes them along is not the thunderous noise of a jet, nor the pressure of a Niagara. It's a quiet energy that you sense even if you can't see it.

—GORDON MACDONALD[3]

God has honored that decision to listen to my passion. He continues to take that thread and weave it through my life in ways I could not have imagined. Other people have confirmed my calling, but the greatest affirmation I have is the intense joy and peace that settles over me when I have been with a group of women, operating in the strength of my passion and gifts. I sense the presence of God, and I bask in His pleasure.

Your Passion

Now how do we get you to your passion? Take some time with the next questions. Write out your answers and ask the Lord to come and lead your thoughts and remembrances. You may not settle the answer today, but you will begin pursuing the heart of God and His response to you.

- Think about your childhood and your teenage years.
  What did you really enjoy doing?
  Who did you like to be with?
  Were you the leader, the instigator, or the follower?
  Someone has said that the very things that got us in trouble as children are often the strengths that are admired in us as adults. Did you get in trouble for talking too much? Asking too many questions? Taking things apart and putting them back together? Mull over your youth and identify your joy.

- How does the joy of your youth translate into the adult world?

- What things/activities/callings give you great excitement and yet provide peace?

- What makes you really, really glad (apart from clean, sweet kids and a good night's sleep)?

- What do people tell you that you are good at?

- What do you dream about?

- Are you spending any part of your life devoted to these passions?

- Does your life today encourage your passions, or does it frustrate who you are really meant to be?

- If God were calling you to change, could you? Are you afraid to try new things, content to yearn from a distance?

What do you want? Don't minimize it; don't try to make sure it sounds spiritual; don't worry about whether or not you can obtain it. Just stay with the question until you begin to get an answer. This is the way we keep current with our hearts.

—JOHN ELDREDGE[4]

Inside of you, God has put a passion detector. It's built to go off in the presence of your gladness. Some of us can't sleep in the presence of passion. Some of our hearts begin to beat rapidly. Some of us can't stop talking about that thing we love. Have you heard it go off lately? When? Where? Why? If it has been a while since you were roused by the alarm of passion, retrace your steps, find your way back, and pray for God's leading. He knows the way. He will direct your path. He longs for you to know your passion.

But What About My Family?

Knowing your passion and pursuing it requires listening to God. Your passions, your marriage, and your children can all work together. Read Jan Johnson's insight from her book *Living a Purpose-full Life:*

> But how do we act on the God-given purposes in our lives and still be attentive, caring wives and mothers? First, we abandon the idea that God has designed life so family is separate from service and that the two must compete. In a speech at the 1997 Women's Ministries Symposium, Jill Briscoe talked about the fallacy of having a hierarchy of priorities, such as (1) God, (2) husband, (3) children, (4) church, and so on. Instead, she suggested, there's a hierarchy of principles—"God and his kingdom come first. God will tell you what is front and center today. Are you listening?"
>
> If you're a praying person who listens to God and looks into the hearts of people around you, obeying the first and second commandments to love God and love others (Matthew 22:37-39), you'll know when to skip the day's entire to-do list and take your kids to the beach, take yourself to the beach, take your Bible to the beach, or take your kids and your neighbor's lonely, autistic son to the beach. If each day is about knowing and loving God, that day's activities will flow out of a divine common sense. In fact, you'll probably know beforehand because God will have been nudging you for quite some time.

Jan goes on to say:

> Contrary to what some people may believe, a woman doesn't have to choose between having a purpose in life and being a faithful and fun-loving mom, wife, and friend. One of the best things we can contribute to the people we love is to be a woman who responds to the call of God. Through us, those we love experience the joy of following God and are often challenged to consider their own God-infused purposes.[5]

Now What?

You have named your passions and embraced your purpose. You are motivated by the excitement and inspired by the call of God in your life. You are ready to dive in, and then the baby crawls by with a "stink bomb" or your fourth-grader yells, "What's a good sentence with the word 'annex'?" Reality check.

That's why I named this chapter "Passionate Contentment." The Lord has given me the privilege of motherhood, and yet He has burned a deep passion for ministry into my heart. For me, the key to balancing my calling and these years of mothering is to continue to feed the passion and yet rest in His holy contentment for these days.

But godliness with contentment is great gain.

—1 TIMOTHY 6:6

There are days that I will be away with women and teach and interact until my cup of gladness is full. A day full of passionate ministry. And then there are days at home when I can't remember if I have ever been called to anything else. I am just the mommy: faithful boo-boo kisser ... faithful preparer of food ... faithful carpool driver. A different cup is full of gladness, and I go to bed at night and hold onto the thread: a day of passionate contentment.

These days of mothering are very, very good days. I do not want to miss even one. And yet I do not want to lose the passion that was given to me. I want to agree with the apostle Paul when he writes in Philippians 4:11-13:

> I have learned to be content whatever the circumstances. I know what it is to be in need, and I know what it is to have plenty. I have learned the secret of being content in any and every situation, whether well fed or hungry, whether living in plenty or in want. I can do everything through him who gives me strength.

What did Paul mean by "I have learned the secret of being content"? He had learned that he could trust God. He could trust God's timing and His methods. He could trust God's provision and His leading. When we are fully devoted to Jesus, trusting in His promises for our lives, we are covered with an outpouring of contentment. We can hold onto the thread of our passion and recite Philippians 1:6 with complete confidence: "He who began a good work in you will carry it on to completion until the day of Christ Jesus."

We can know with assurance that the work He began, the passion and calling that burns inside us, is being guarded and protected. Your purpose is God's *good* work in you. He will complete the work He has begun in your soul. He will take the thread of passion and weave a tapestry.

As mothers, we sometimes struggle with our passions, believing that to deny them is somehow sacrifical and good. God created you and called you with a purpose. To deny your passions is to reject His call on your life.

But what about contentment? Without contentment, you may wish your life away, longing for the activities of life's next season, missing the glory of God's purpose in today.

Contentment is not freedom from desire, but freedom of desire. Being content is not pretending that everything is the way you wish it would be; it is not acting as though you have no wishes. Rather, it is no longer being ruled by your desires.

—JOHN ELDREDGE[6]

Passionate contentment is about cultivating your gifts, enjoying your passions, and yet resting. Passionate contentment keeps you from arriving at the end of your life and sitting down to write an essay that begins, "If I had my life to live over ..." Instead, because your passion has been sown with contentment, you are free to begin today and write an essay that begins, "I have my whole life before me ... " Put words to your longings. Dream big. Surprise yourself with the musings of your soul.

Paul writes in Philippians 3:12, "Not that I have already

obtained all this, or have already been made perfect, but I press on to take hold of that for which Christ Jesus took hold of me." Then in verse 14, "I press on toward the goal to win the prize for which God has called me heavenward in Christ Jesus."

I wrote out this passage a long time ago, and the faded piece of paper hangs by little bits of tape to the wall over my desk. I ask myself almost every day, *Why did Jesus take hold of you?* And then I remind myself, *Get your eyes on heaven and press on.*

Turn your eyes toward heaven. Jesus took hold of you for a purpose. Let Him give wings to your passions, live according to holy contentment, and in all these things ... press on.

Be merciful,

just as your Father is merciful.

LUKE 6:36

Chapter Ten

Someone to Run Beside

oday has been a very lonely day for me. I have felt misunderstood at almost every turn. Every place that I looked in my home made me feel overwhelmed, shouting to me that I am a family management failure. I lay on my face this morning and rambled before the Lord. I am sure He smiled as His weary daughter came into His presence and then wouldn't sit still. I put a frozen lasagna in the oven tonight and heard "the list" whisper to me that my children deserve better. I called Paul at work for consoling. He tried to empathize, and, bless him, he tried to fix. He wanted to call somebody and get the situation straightened out. I love him for wanting to try, but I couldn't be fixed today, so I hung up and still felt terribly alone.

I wallowed in the frustration of my inadequacy until the Lord led me to call a friend. Not just any friend, mind you, but a woman who has permission to walk around in my soul.

She listened. She agreed with me. She picked up my burden and stood under it with me. She gave me grace and tenderly led me to the mercy of Jesus. She ministered to me, and her words held me with their love. With my burden shared, I was stronger. With my tears dried, I could see clearly. With someone to run beside, I felt my pace quicken and my energy return.

The things that care for my soul include developing intimate friendships with women. Though this issue represents a land-mine of potential pain and confusing history for many of us, myself included, my relationships with other women who share my devotion to God are essential elements of nurture in my own soul's life. We know one another's history, we can see trouble signs ahead for one another, we can confess our sins and offer each other the hope and perspective so essential to growth.

—MINDY CALIGUIRE[1]

Women are the great caregivers in this world. We scoop up our children when they fall down, and we stand behind them when they face new tests and hard days. We care for our husbands in sickness and in health. We walk beside them through richer and through poorer. We love them in and out of every life season. Of course, we are the recipients of their great love and affection, their protection and provision. But who cares for the caregivers?

I strongly believe that we have been wired, by God, with a deep need for the friendships of women. Women can care for other women with the profound ability that comes from affinity and experience, from understanding and familiarity. It is the kinship of sisterhood; it is God's gift of friendship for a woman's soul.

Where Have All the Friendships Gone?

More and more, I meet women who do not have very close women friends. They cover by saying something like "My husband is my best friend" or "My best friend moved away and we lost touch." One of the greatest things I ever did for my marriage was to stop trying to make Paul into my girlfriend. It has probably saved our marriage, and I know that Paul is relieved. He never could get the whole effort quite right, and we both would be frustrated. I mean, he doesn't really care about paint colors or fabric swatches. He wants to care because he loves me and knows they are important to me, but he never could get into the joy of the process.

Paul is ready to stop after one or two fabric options, but a girlfriend will drive 70 miles with you to get a swatch of fabric and make a day of it with lunch and a stop at the outlet mall. At a more emotional level, Paul is content to process a discussion one or two times. I might need to talk something through 40 times, and a girlfriend always seems to listen with fresh ears and a willing heart. The truth is that women with great husbands still need the friendships of women, and women with distant husbands need them even more.

Sometimes I wish I had been born earlier. I don't long for

the days of washing clothes on rocks down by the creek, but I long for the fellowship that those women had, the shared work and shared hearts. Women used to work together in the fields; cook, clean, and sew together; and raise their children together. They taught one another and kept each other accountable. I joke with Paul that I would be a great candidate for commune living; I yearn for shared community.

But we live in the days of autonomy. Everyone has become separate and independent. I am sure there are some benefits, but have we sacrificed the joy of community and deep friendships?

When we were in Florida, we lived for a year and a half across the street from a woman I never met. If I was in the front yard with the children, I would hear her garage door going up and then see her car coming. She never looked at me or my waving children, and she did not get out of her car until her garage door was safely down. She kept her miniblinds drawn and sent her children to the mailbox and out with the garbage. It became a huge joke in our family. "Maybe she's in a witness protection program," we'd say. But beyond the joke, it was a sad commentary on today's world. We have become separated, cut off, and we just want everyone to leave us alone.

We have pulled our blinds tightly and built tall fences around our homes and our hearts. Friends used to sit on the front porch to talk. Then they moved inside to sit numbly in front of the television. And now, there isn't even a need to gather. One can sit all alone in a darkened room in front of a flickering screen, never saying a real word to anyone, and click all over the world. We used to be connected to people. Now we are just connected to a web.

Where have all the friendships gone? I think they have been replaced by more activity, longer hours at work, the

World Wide Web, and pure exhaustion. We have a career path, financial goals, children to raise, and retirement plans, and we are doing it all alone, as quickly as possible. The heart yearns for friendship, but our busy lives don't leave much room for the time required to cultivate depth and intimacy.

Someone to Run Beside

A few years ago my mentor told me that we pace ourselves according to who we run beside. Although the running analogy only applies to my spiritual life, I still like the picture it gives. I am only a runner wanna-be. I wear running shoes because they feel great. Nonetheless, any real marathoner can tell you that it's true. To run beside someone of like heart and stride keeps you well-paced and focused. One runner told me, "I never could have finished a marathon without my running partner. Her constant presence made me more responsible and consistent in my training."

I can think of certain people in my world whose company invigorates me, and when they leave, I am full of resolve, ideas, and intentions about God, self-improvement, and service to others. I can also think of people in my world whose presence exhausts me. And when they leave, I am ready for a long, long nap.
—GORDON MACDONALD[2]

God has sent several great women into my life to spiritually run alongside me. Each has come to me in a different season and caused me to run a little faster. These women share my passion to know God intimately and pursue Him with intentional living and purpose. These women have caused me to pick up my spiritual pace, inspiring me, adding to my energy, challenging me to change and grow, settling my heart, and bringing real peace into my life. These women are soul mates, sent by God to help me look more like Him and less like me. To run beside them is a privilege—God's tender mercy for my soul.

Kindred Hearts

I am not sure the depth of spiritual life that I desire can be sought apart from a kindred heart. I need a safe place to process all the goofy thoughts I have and a partner who will quicken my spiritual steps. I need the comfort and accountability of someone close and the power of togetherness and the energy that comes from connection. I have many levels of that relationship with my husband, but there is something special about the kindred heart of another woman.

Jan Johnson calls these kindred hearts "partner friendships" and describes them like this:

> This sort of friendship goes beyond the normal, helpful conversations about where to find what you need on sale or how to get kids to do their homework. It involves walking alongside someone, listening to another woman, forging a union of minds, persevering together, and being transparent. These friendships nurture our passion. In such friendships, people listen

to each other, making observations and asking questions such as these:

- What is God calling you to do?
- What are your hopes, your deepest desires?
- Have you noticed how much you talk about this purpose?
- How are you managing your purposes in regard to family and work?
- What are your motives? Do they honor God?[3]

Through different seasons of my life, I can trace my spiritual growth to the influence of godly women who have come alongside me.

In my junior year of college, God sent Michele. Michele and I pledged the same sorority and then became fast friends and roommates. I was a growing believer in those years, but Michele made me pick up the pace. I can still vividly remember Michele getting ready to go out and then sitting with her Bible to read and to pray before her date came to pick her up. That picture of a woman preparing her body and her soul to be beautiful has stuck with me. Her quiet example challenged me to invite the Lord into every area of my life and to seek Him with great fervency.

After college, Michele and I spent a month in Europe, the generous graduation gift of our parents, and made enough memories to fill up a lifetime. A year later, I knew that the Lord was calling me to Dallas, Texas, for seminary, and Michele said, "I might like to go with you and be your roommate." I was absolutely thrilled. We planned a weekend trip to Dallas to check out the big city. The whole time there, I knew that Michele was considering whether this move would be God's will for her. Our jam-packed weekend came to an end, and we headed to DFW to catch our flight home. Standing in line at the gate, a girl tapped Michele on the shoulder.

"Michele Miller? Do you remember me? We had a class together at Carolina."

"Yes. Oh, my goodness. How fun to see you."

Michele and her friend chatted, and I remember thinking, *How cool to see someone you know in a place that you have never been.* After we settled into our seats, Michele said, "I'm moving with you to Dallas."

"You are? How do you know for sure?"

"Well, I cast a fleece."

"You did a what?"

"This is such a huge decision for me. I told God that I needed His help. I asked Him to let me see someone I know while we were in Dallas if it was His will for me to come with you."

"You told God that? But you don't know anybody here."

"I know, and I thought up until a few minutes ago that I wasn't going to come with you. When my friend tapped me on the shoulder, I knew it was from God."

Cold chills. I had never heard of such faith before. I remember saying something to Michele about being bossy with God. But she hadn't been bossy. She had been humbly seeking His will with a pure heart to serve Him and go where He called. I am sure that He answered her fleece—like Gideon's fleece in Judges 6:36-40—because of her great faith.

That summer, Michele moved with me to Dallas, where she bought a car, got a job, and eventually met the man who became her husband. She lives in Canada now with her pastor husband and their three children. From the great distance between us, I still run beside my dear friend. We visit, e-mail, talk on the phone, and pray for each other. I am committed to a lifetime of friendship. I look more like Jesus because Michele came along and made me pick up my spiritual pace.

About 10 years ago at the time I'm writing this, God brought a woman into my life who has rocked my world. My friend Nicole, a gifted actress, author, and friend, is one of the most amazing women I have ever known. We live in totally different worlds. I am a mom; Nicole is not. Nicole is a coffee connoisseur; I drink hot chocolate. She is a runner; I am a walker. I am at home every day; Nicole travels all over the country. Two days ago, we talked while she was in Los Angeles; today she e-mailed me from Connecticut. But in spite of every difference, God has knit our hearts together at the deepest places of friendship ... soul to soul.

Nicole is one of those women who takes your breath

True friends don't spend time gazing into each other's eyes. They show great tenderness toward each other, but they face in the same direction—toward common projects, interests, goals—above all, toward a common Lord.

—C. S. Lewis[4]

away. She can have more really solid ideas in about five minutes than most of us have in five years. She loves Jesus and pursues Him with all of her being. She is quick-witted, generous, highly creative, and irresistibly fun. She is always learning, reading, dreaming, and becoming. Nicole makes me want more of Jesus and challenges my socks off while encouraging me as few others can.

Nicole and I have to work at our friendship. We have to schedule dates months in advance. We make appointments to talk on the phone. We plan when we will see each other again and juggle schedules to make it happen. We send e-mail, leave messages, and write notes. Nicole will fly in a few days early when she's in my area or stay a few days longer. When that won't work, she has flown me to where she is or taken me with her. We have driven halfway between any two points on a map just to have breakfast and a few hours together. Our friendship is a commitment for both of us, but the sacrifice and energy it takes is multiplied a hundredfold in my soul.

More recently, the Lord has reconnected me with another woman of kindred heart. Mindy Caliguire is the wife of a seminary friend. I first met Mindy when she came out to visit her fiancé and stayed with me for the week. There was an immediate kinship that I believe was a divine appointment. We have never lived in the same city, but we are crazy about the same Jesus, and He has given us identical passions for women and for the soul.

Mindy is a wife and the mother of three boys. She is a writer, editor, and teacher. From her passion about soul care came a publishing company that is reaching believers and unbelievers with the message of spiritual health through Jesus. She is real and vulnerable, a thinker, and a pray-er. I am so thankful to call her my friend.

When I talk to Mindy, we almost speak the same words after each other. We are so excited to connect and get to deeper places that our small amounts of time run out too quickly. There is always more to talk about, more to consider, or more to pray about. Mindy mirrors for me what a godly mother looks like ... in process ... pursuing God ... caring for her soul ... giving and living grace ... passionate and yet content.

One early morning, after a night of delayed flights, little sleep, and a long drive, Nicole got to my house around 7:00 A.M. We did the happy dance and laughed unto tears to finally be face-to-face. Making our way into the kitchen, I asked, "What

Soul care happens only in a community of people on a journey to God, only in a group of people who turn their chairs toward each other. Spiritual friends are people filled with Christ's energy who have turned their chairs, who pour their passions into each other and invite others to join them on the porch. But not many people ... have one truly spiritual friend.

—Larry Crabb[5]

can I get you to drink?" Without missing a beat, Nicole said, "I don't care if we drink dishwater as long as I'm with you." *Yes*, my soul sighed. With kindred hearts, the world falls away and the food of great friendship nourishes the hungry soul.

All my kindred hearts live hundreds and even thousands of miles away. I have questioned the Lord's arrangement time and time again, wondering why I can't have a kindred heart next door or even across town. My only solace is believing that their distance will keep me mindful of their treasure. Maybe I will nurture our friendship with greater tenderness because I am reminded so often that a woman to run beside is precious and rare.

Who Is Beside You?

Do you have someone to run beside? Do you have a woman in your life who causes you to pick up the pace? Look around and see who is beside you. Who are you pacing yourself with? Do you have a soul mate beside you or someone you need to distance yourself from? Are you being held back in the pack of "slow runners" when your soul longs to pull away from the herd and quicken the pace?

Many years ago, there was a woman in my life who had decided that she was going to be my friend. She was a sweet person who loved the Lord, but we lacked a real soul connection. This woman called me almost every day, and because I was lonely at home with my first baby, I began to embrace her as a friend. Never mind that her attitude was dismal and depressing. Never mind that our theologies took divergent paths. Never mind that she was miserable in her marriage and in life. Never mind that her walk with the Lord was shallow and sporadic.

Over time I began to open up my heart to this woman,

until one day she was sitting in my home, giving me very commanding advice about my life. I remember disconnecting from the conversation long enough to think, *Who am I listening to? This is the most graceless stuff I've ever heard. Why am I letting someone who is not passionate about Jesus speak into my life?* I finally woke up that day and realized that this friendship was not healthy for me. This woman could be in my life, but I would not give her permission to walk around in my soul.

Proverbs 4:23 says, "Above all else, guard your heart, for it is the wellspring of life." Guarding my heart meant that I had to ask myself, *Whom will I give permission to speak into my life?* The "wellspring" in this passage refers to our actions, our responses, and our attitudes—what comes out of us. I made a commitment to protect my heart because so much is decided there—my attitude toward my husband, the parenting and care of my children, my view of the world, and most importantly, my relationship with my Savior.

Guarding my heart forced me to distance my soul from this woman and replace her input with godly wisdom and counsel. I decided to spend less time with her and consciously did not ask for her advice. I began to examine my casual friendships and chose godly women for insight and direction. Caring for my soul meant that I had to guard my heart, choosing who had permission to walk there.

My questions for you are:

- Who has permission to walk around in your life and give counsel?

- Do those friendships hinder your walk with the Lord, or do they spur you on toward greater godliness? Do they make you run faster or just make you tired?

- What steps can you take today to move toward healthy friendships?

- Do you have a kindred friend in your world?

- Do you treasure that friendship and nurture it?

- What can you do to bless her? Do you remember that she is God's gift for your soul?

Finishing Well

I said to you earlier that more than almost anything, I want to finish well. What that means for me is this: I want to go through my whole life as a devoted follower of Christ. I don't want to stop and start over and over again. I want to be learning and improving until Jesus comes to get me. I want to change—really change—and grow through the years, living a pure faith built on the lessons of God's grace.

I want to love Paul for my whole life. I want our marriage to evolve and grow. I want to move from just knowing him into embracing what I know about him. I want to love the quirks and celebrate our differences. I want my love for him to increase and mature. I want to wake up at 80, roll over and look at my bridegroom, and know that I have loved one man well.

I want to be a godly mother all the way until the end. I don't want to burn out and spend the last 20 years of my life in an RV detached from my family, trying to find all the things I think I missed. I want my children to know the blessing of a mom who really loves Jesus and models for them until death the pursuit of holiness and grace.

I want my whole life to be fueled by the passions and purpose that God put inside my heart.

I am just a woman, talking a big dream, but the reality is, having someone to run beside is an integral part of my finishing well. If it weren't for the godly women in my life, I'd be tempted to quit more often, stay down longer, and give up more than I start. Ecclesiastes 4:9-12 puts it like this:

Two are better than one, because they have a good return for their work: If one falls down, his friend can help him up. But pity the man who falls and has no one to help him up! Also, if two lie down together, they will keep warm. But how can one keep warm alone? Though one may be overpowered, two can defend themselves. A cord of three strands is not quickly broken.

The world tries to separate us, but God keeps trying to put us together. He built the church for the community of believers to come for worship and fellowship. Jesus gathered 12 men around Him for training. Why didn't He just go to them one at a time and train them for a few months each? Because they needed the gift of each other. They needed the experience of shared struggle, iron sharpening iron, and kindred hearts. He later sent them out in twos because again they needed the companionship and accountability; they needed one another to remind them of the vision and the call; they needed deep friendship to finish well.

If you are a mother who longs for godliness and passion, you desperately need someone to run beside. You need a kindred heart—someone who is committed to soul care, someone who lives in the tender mercy of God's grace, a woman in process like you, with her eyes set firmly on her Savior. You need a sister for the journey ... someone to pace yourself with ... someone who makes you run a little faster ... someone who is committed to finishing well.

Only surrender your soul to the godly. Protect the treasure and the passion that God has put within you. Pray for His leading and provision.

May you know the tender mercy of Jesus in the gift of a kindred heart for your soul.

Keep yourselves in God's love as you

wait for the mercy

of our Lord Jesus Christ

to bring you to eternal life.

JUDE 21

A Mother's Prayer

O Father,

Holiness seems so far from me, and yet it is truly the desire of my heart. I long for intimacy. I long to know You. I want my whole life to reflect Your presence and Your power. I want to live astounded by Your grace and Your glory.

And yet, God, it's just me. Fragile and sinful me. Come and make me Yours. Heal my wounds. Forgive my old sins, again. Give new words to my prayers. Restore my yearning for truth. Feed me with Your insight and wisdom. Cover me with Your lavish love.

I want this man and these children to live in the blessing of a spiritually healthy woman. Let me be that woman. Remove the distractions that keep me from godliness. Step into the blur of my life rushing by and speak stillness into my days. Hold me close and care for my soul.

In these years of mothering, let me choose to surrender the place of my soul for Your safekeeping. Whisper to my heart and give direction to my steps. Shout to me from Your vastness and add wisdom to my words. Let me love and celebrate life from the full cup of Your grace and peace.

Thank You, my Savior, my Keeper, my Friend, for the tender mercy that comes and fills my soul. In the precious name of Jesus, amen.

Acknowledgments

I will run into people I have known in the grocery store. After they look through the maze of mini-grocery carts, four dancing children, and boxes of cereal flying off the shelves, they zero in on my face and ask in a curious but pensive tone, "Are these all yours?"

I want to say, "Nope, I like to bring a lot of people with me to ask me for things. They help me buy stuff that's not on my list, and they keep me confused and distracted for most of the time that we are here." Instead, I smile and say, "Yes."

"How old are they?"

"Two, four, six, and ten."

And then the next question is almost always, "Don't you write books? When do you find time to write?"

My honest answer is that I don't exactly know how the writing gets done, except that I have a husband who believes in me more than I will ever believe in myself.

My deepest gratitude goes to my husband, Paul. Thank you for every night that you fed, bathed, and put the children to bed while I hid in the library with my laptop. Thank you for giving me almost every one of your days off for the past year. Thank you for enduring with enthusiasm and steadfast love. You are my blessing. You are the only reason that I am able to write. I love you.

Thank you to my precious children, Taylor, Grayson, William, and AnnaGrace. You make it fun to wake up every day. Mommy is done now. Let's do the happy dance.

Thank you to my parents, Joe and Novie Thomas, for the strong gifts of love and family. Thank you to my family and friends who have prayed me through this book: Ima Thomas, Craig and Kim Thomas, April and Amanda, J.T. and Jodi Thomas, Jerry and Carlye Arnold, Michele Pelton, Laura Johnson, Jill Schaefer, and Two Rivers Church.

Three of my dearest friends read through parts of this manuscript at different stages, giving me tremendous input and wisdom. Thank you to Mindy Caliguire, Nicole Johnson, and Jim Smith. Your words of encouragement talked me back to sanity time and again. You each make me run faster toward the Father.

Thank you, Jennifer Cortez, for believing in the vision and message of this book. Your professional support has been invaluable to me in these years, but your friendship has become the greater blessing. Welcome to the land of Mommy!

Thank you to Liz Duckworth for the gift of editing. Thank you, Julie Kuss and Stacey Herebic, for the enthusiasm and heart you have brought to this project. Thank you, Mark Maddox, for the opportunity to come alongside the integrity and ministry of Focus on the Family.

And to my sweet Jesus, I am completely amazed and humbled by Your grace and love for me. Please take this work and use it for Your glory. Use these pages to draw moms to Yourself. Make sure that people know more about You and less about me because of these words. Thank You for my precious family. The life You have already given to me is exceedingly abundantly beyond all I could have ever asked for or imagined.

Reading List

From Fear to Freedom: Living as Sons and Daughters of God,
Rose Marie Miller, Harold Shaw Publishers, ©1994.

*The Call: Finding and Fulfilling the Central Purpose of Your
Life,* Os Guinness, Word Publishers, ©1998.

The Unknown God, Alistair McGrath, Eerdmans, ©1999.

A Christian's Secret of a Happy Life, Hannah Whitall Smith,
Revell, ©1985.

Fresh Brewed Life, Nicole Johnson, Thomas Nelson, ©1999.

Write for Your Soul: The Whys and Hows of Journaling, Jeff
and Mindy Caliguire, Soul Care Communications, ©1998.

Gift from the Sea, Anne Morrow Lindbergh, Pantheon
Books, ©1955.

Celebration of Discipline, Richard Foster, Harper & Row,
©1978.

Prayer, E. M. Bounds, Whitaker House, ©1997.

What Happens When Women Pray, Evelyn Christenson,
Victor Books, ©1975.

God Guides, Mary Geegh, Missionary Press, ©1970.

Ordering Your Private World, Gordon MacDonald, Thomas Nelson, ©1985.

Restoring Your Spiritual Passion, Gordon MacDonald, Thomas Nelson, ©1986.

Living a Purpose-full Life, Jan Johnson, WaterBrook, ©1999.

The Journey of Desire, John Eldredge, Thomas Nelson, ©2000.

The Wonder of It All, Bryan Chapell, Crossway, ©1999.

Notes

Chapter 1

1. Janet Lanese, *Mothers Are Like Miracles* (New York: Fireside, 1998), p. 80.
2. Quoted in *Mothers Are Like Miracles,* p. 85.

Chapter 2

1. Bryan Chapell, *The Wonder of It All* (Wheaton, Ill.: Crossway Books, 1999), p. 139.
2. John Eldredge *The Journey of Desire* (Nashville: Thomas Nelson, 2000), p. 193.
3. Ibid., p. 194.

Chapter 3

1. John Eldredge *The Journey of Desire* (Nashville: Thomas Nelson, 2000), p. 181.

Chapter 4

1. Bryan Chapell, *The Wonder of It All* (Wheaton, Ill.: Crossway Books, 1999), p. 41.
2. Jill Briscoe, Focus on the Family broadcast.
3. Chapell, *The Wonder of It All,* p. 20.

Chapter 5

1. Michael Quoist, *With Open Heart,* as quoted by Gordon MacDonald in *Restoring Your Spiritual Passion* (Nashville: Thomas Nelson, 1986), p. 123.
2. MacDonald, *Restoring Your Spiritual Passion,* p. 26.
3. Jill Briscoe, speaking at a conference.
4. Jill Briscoe, speaking at a conference.
5. Oswald Chambers, *My Utmost for His Highest* (New York: Dodd, Mead, 1935), June 26 reading, p. 178.
6. Mary Geegh, *God Guides* (Holland, Mich.: Missionary Press, 1970), p. 1.

Chapter 6

1. Gordon MacDonald, *Restoring Your Spiritual Passion* (Nashville: Thomas Nelson, 1986), p. 37.
2. Madeleine L'Engle, *Walking on Water* (New York: North Point Press, 1980), p. 12.
3. Gordon MacDonald, *Ordering Your Private World* (Nashville: Thomas Nelson, 1985), p. 141.

Chapter 7

1. Quoted by Joanna Weaver in *Having a Mary Heart in a Martha World* (Colorado Springs, Colo.: WaterBrook, 2000), p. 145.
2. Bryan Chapell, *The Wonder of It All* (Wheaton, Ill.: Crossway Books, 1999), p. 154.
3. Jack Miller, quoted by Scotty Smith in *Speechless* (Grand Rapids, Mich.: Zondervan, 1999), p. 127.

Chapter 8

1. Alister McGrath, *The Unknown God* (Grand Rapids, Mich.: Eerdmans, 1999), p. 112.

Chapter 9

1. John Eldredge, *The Journey of Desire* (Nashville: Thomas Nelson, 2000), p. 164.
2. Bill and Kathy Peel, quoted by Jan Johnson in *Living a Purpose-full Life* (Colorado Springs, Colo.: WaterBrook 1999), p. 43.
3. Gordon MacDonald, *Restoring Your Spiritual Passion* (Nashville: Thomas Nelson, 1986), p. 218.
4. Eldredge, *The Journey of Desire*, p. 168.
5. Johnson, *Living a Purpose-full Life*, pp. 179-80, 186.
6. Eldredge, *The Journey of Desire*, p. 182.

Chapter 10

1. Mindy Caliguire, personal correspondence.
2. Gordon MacDonald, *Restoring Your Spiritual Passion* (Nashville: Thomas Nelson, 1986), p. 71.
3. Jan Johnson, *Living a Purpose-full Life* (Colorado Springs, Colo.: WaterBrook, 1999), pp. 135-36.
4. Quoted in *Friends*, Ellyn Sanna, comp. (Uhrichsville, Ohio: Barbour House Publishing, 1999), p. 39.
5. Larry Crabb, *The Safest Place on Earth* (Nashville: Word, 1999), p. 183.

About the Author

Angela lives in Tennessee with her husband, Paul, and their children: Taylor, Grayson, William, and AnnaGrace. She is a full-time mom, part-time author, and conference speaker. Angela is a graduate of the University of North Carolina at Chapel Hill and Dallas Theological Seminary. Angela has some hobbies, but now she mostly folds clothes in her spare time.

To contact Angela, please visit her Web site at:
www.angelaguffey.com
or e-mail her at:
Angela@angelaguffey.com

To inquire about speaking engagements with Angela at your church or event please contact Creative Trust at 615-297-5010 or send an information request to info@creativetrust.com.

Also by Angela Thomas Guffey:
Prayers for Expectant Mothers
Prayers for New Mothers

FOCUS ON THE FAMILY®

*W*elcome to the *F*amily!

Whether you received this book as a gift, borrowed it from
a friend, or purchased it yourself, we're glad you read it! It's just
one of the many helpful, insightful and encouraging
resources produced by Focus on the Family.

In fact, that's what Focus on the Family is all about—providing inspiration, information and biblically based advice to people in all stages of life.

It began in 1977 with the vision of one man, Dr. James Dobson, a licensed
psychologist and author of 16 best-selling books on marriage, parenting,
and family. Alarmed by the societal, political, and economic pressures
that were threatening the existence of the American family, Dr. Dobson
founded Focus on the Family with one employee—an assistant—
and a once-a-week radio broadcast, aired on only 36 stations.

Now an international organization, Focus on the Family is dedicated
to preserving Judeo-Christian values and strengthening the family
through more than 70 different ministries, including eight separate
daily radio broadcasts; television public service announcements;
11 publications; and a steady series of books and award-winning
films and videos for people of all ages and interests.

Recognizing the needs of, as well as the sacrifices and important
contribution made by, such diverse groups as educators, physicians,
attorneys, crisis pregnancy center staff and single parents,
Focus on the Family offers specific outreaches to uphold and
minister to these individuals, too. And it's all done for one purpose,
and one purpose only: to encourage and strengthen individuals
and families through the life-changing message of Jesus Christ.

• • •

For more information about the ministry, or if we can be of help to your
family, simply write to Focus on the Family, Colorado Springs, CO 80995
or call 1-800-A-FAMILY (1-800-232-6459). Friends in Canada may write
Focus on the Family, P.O. Box 9800, Stn. Terminal, Vancouver, B.C. V6B 4G3
or call 1-800-661-9800. Visit our Web site—www.family.org—
to learn more about Focus on the Family or to find out if
there is an associate office in your country.

We'd love to hear from you!

Try These Other Faith-Strengthening Resources
From Focus on the Family®

Then God Created Woman

Through examples of various stages of a woman's life, *Then God Created Woman* explores the search for wholeness that all women experience and seek to find in relationships. The author explores ways of achieving godly femininity through a loving relationship with God, forgiveness (healing from damaged relationships), giving God control, maturing spiritually, understanding men, finding freedom in sexuality, and knowing God.

Renewed Hearts, Changed Lives

Renewed Hearts, Changed Lives is a compilation of true stories from women who were inspired to examine their faith and draw nearer to God while attending Focus on the Family's Renewing the Heart conferences. You'll be encouraged as you read how these women discovered God's unwavering grace and steadfast love in the midst of trials and trying times.

Kindred Hearts

Written by a mother of two grown daughters and based on her experiences, *Kindred Hearts* is designed to strengthen the bond between mothers and daughters. The book promotes activities like letter writing and Scripture exploration—to help understand why mothers and daughters are the way they are—and features quotes from famous authors about motherhood.

●   ●   ●

To request these or other resources, or for information on Renewing the Heart Women's Ministries, simply call 1-800-A-FAMILY, or write to Focus on the Family, Colorado Springs, CO 80995. Friends in Canada may call 1-800-661-9800 or write Focus on the Family, P.O. Box 9800, Stn. Terminal, Vancouver, B.C. V6B 4G3. Visit our Web site—www.renewingtheheart.com—to learn more about Renewing the Heart Women's Ministries.